Physical Characteristics of the American Pit Bull Terrier
(from the United Kennel Club breed standard)

Back: Short and strong. Slightly sloping from withers to rump. Slightly arched at loins, which should be slightly tucked.

Weight: Not important. Females preferred from 30 to 50 pounds. Males from 35 to 60 pounds.

Tail: Short in comparison to size. Set low and tapering to a fine point. Not carried over back.

Ribs: Close. Well-sprung, with deep back ribs.

Thigh: Long with muscles developed. Hocks down and straight.

Coat: Glossy. Short and stiff to the touch.

Color: Any color or marking permissible.

American Pit Bull Terrier

by F. Favorito

9 **History of the** American Pit Bull Terrier

Uncover the background of this popular and versatile breed. Learn about the theories of its origin, its original purpose as a fighting dog, the breeders who established and registered the breed and the variations in type among today's Pit Bulls.

19 **Characteristics of the** American Pit Bull Terrier

Delve beneath the media hype and notoriety to get to know the real Pit Bull and acquaint yourself with the breed's wonderful personality traits and many abilities. A companion beyond compare, the Pit Bull offers a world of potential to a responsible owner who takes the time and effort to develop his dog properly.

33 **Breed Standard for the** American Pit Bull Terrier

Learn the requirements of a well-bred American Pit Bull Terrier by studying the description of the breed as set forth in the United Kennel Club's breed standard. Both show dogs and pets must possess key characteristics as outlined in the breed standard.

39 **Your Puppy** American Pit Bull Terrier

Be advised about choosing a reputable breeder and selecting a healthy, typical puppy. Understand the responsibilities of ownership, including home preparation, acclimatization, the vet and prevention of common puppy problems.

58 **Everyday Care of Your** American Pit Bull Terrier

Enter into a sensible discussion of dietary and feeding considerations, exercise, grooming, traveling and identification of your dog. This chapter discusses American Pit Bull Terrier care for all stages of development.

69 **Training Your** American Pit Bull Terrier

By Charlotte Schwartz
Be informed about the importance of training your American Pit Bull Terrier from the basics of housebreaking and understanding the development of a young dog to executing obedience commands (sit, stay, down, etc.).

Contents

KENNEL CLUB BOOKS® AMERICAN PIT BULL TERRIER
ISBN 13: 978-1-59378-202-3

Copyright © 2003, 2009 • Kennel Club Books® A Division of BowTie, Inc.
40 Broad Street, Freehold, New Jersey 07728 USA
Cover Design Patented: US 6,435,559 B2 • Printed in South Korea

Photographs by:

Norvia Behling, Carolina Biological Supply, T. J. Calhoun, Liza Clancy, Wil de Veer, Doskocil, Isabelle Français, James Hayden-Yoav, James R. Hayden, RBP, Bill Jonas, Dwight R. Kuhn, Dr. Dennis Kunkel, Nancy Liguori, Mikki Pet Products, Phototake, Jean Claude Revy, Dr. Andrew Spielman, Nikki Sussman and C. James Webb.

The publisher wishes to thank all of the owners of the dogs featured in this book.

The exact origin of the American Pit Bull Terrier is in doubt. Theories purport that it derived from either the Staffordshire Bull Terrier or the English Bulldog.

History of the American Pit Bull Terrier

THE GENESIS OF THE BREED IN ITS HOMELAND

Americans like to think of the Pit Bull, or, more properly, the American Pit Bull Terrier, as being a breed of purely American origin. To a large extent, this is true. After all, it was in the United States that this breed took on its definitive form, ability and character. As there are no written records that clearly document the origin of the breed, disagreement among its advocates abounds. Most American Pit Bull historians feel that the American Pit Bull Terrier is the American expression of the game-bred Stafford or Staffordshire Bull Terrier of the United Kingdom. These breed fanciers maintain that as English, and especially Irish, immigrants to the United States established themselves throughout the New World, the little dogs that they prized so highly at home, the game-bred Staffords, sometimes traveled with them. Separated from their foundation stock, the gene pool of Staffordshire Bull Terriers in the United States became more distinct and was subject to the changes imposed by the thinking of American dog breeders, the most obvious of these changes being an increase in size.

Other Pit Bull fanciers have a different opinion regarding the origin of the breed. These fanciers feel that the Pit Bull is a modern-day expression of the original English Bulldog. They speculate that, unlike the Staffordshire Bull Terrier, a breed of known bull-and-terrier ancestry, the Pit Bull has no terrier blood in it at all, but rather is a continuation of the pure Bulldog of Elizabethan days.

SIZE INCREASE

Some feel that the increased size found among American Pit Bulls was originally a response to new demands placed upon the breed in the New World. It is speculated that as "catch work" (catching free-range domesticated animals on large farms and ranches) was added to the breed's duties in America, greater size was selected for in order to allow the breed to serve well in a number of roles. This theory is best represented in the writings of the American purebred dog historian Carl Semencic.

They further speculate that the very obvious differences between the modern show dog known as the Bulldog and the Pit Bull reflect the vastly different purposes for which each was bred, showing versus working. This thinking is best put forth in

the writing of an American historian of the Pit Bull breed, Richard Stratton.

THEORY OF ORIGIN

The author is inclined to agree with the theory that today's American Pit Bull Terrier is the American expression of the Staffordshire Bull Terriers of England and Ireland. Supporting this theory is the fact that the smaller game-bred (fighting stock) American Pit Bull Terriers and the larger game-bred (badger hunting and fighting stock) modern Staffordshire Bull Terriers of England appear to be nearly identical.

Staffordshire Bull Terrier puppy and adult.

ORIGINAL PURPOSE OF THE AMERICAN PIT BULL TERRIER

The specifics of ancient breed history, and the breed's modern reputation notwithstanding, show that there can be no doubt about one thing—and that one thing is the core function of the Pit Bull breed. Throughout the entire existence of the breed, from its earliest days and, to some extent, through modern times, the Pit Bull in its purest working form has been and remains essentially a fighting dog. This is to say that the breed's function, its very purpose, was, and in the minds of some remains, to be a gambler's tool. The breed was originally selectively bred without regard for looks, but rather only for ever-

The American Pit Bull Terrier was never trained to be an attack dog against humans; in fact, Pit Bulls had to be unconditionally loyal and obedient to their handlers, traits they display with their owners today.

increasing ability to fight other Pit Bulls, and *only* other Pit Bulls, in long sustained combat events in man-made dog pits for the enjoyment of human spectators. Note that, unlike some breeds, the Pit Bull's purpose was never to attack man. In fact, it must be noted here that in the organized combat events for which the Pit Bull was and occasionally still is used, these dogs are handled by their human handlers throughout the event. Those who use these dogs in such events have no use for a dog that would in any way endanger the handler rather than its canine opponent.

THE AMERICAN PIT BULL IN THE 20TH CENTURY
While the distant past of the Pit Bull may remain a matter for some disagreement, the more recent history of the breed is indisputable. The breed began the 20th century in its American homeland as a newly officially registered breed. In 1898, a man by the name of Chauncy Bennett began a registry organization called the United Kennel Club (UKC) for the sole purpose of registering the Pit Bull. He did this because the breed had been ignored for registry by the more prestigious American Kennel Club, which was already in existence. The breed has undergone a number of name changes during its years with the United Kennel Club. At one time it was called the Pit Bull Terrier, and at another time the American (Pit) Bull Terrier, but to this day the United Kennel Club still exists and continues to register the breed as the American Pit Bull Terrier. The

The American Pit Bull Terrier has been a registered breed in the US since the creation of the United Kennel Club in 1898.

Pit Bull Terriers, because of their ability to work well with humans and their interesting look, have been used in films and television shows.

UKC has also undergone a number of changes during the course of the century and, although it continues to register the Pit Bull, it registers more breeds today than even the AKC.

Another registry organization in America also began to register the Pit Bull during the very early part of the 20th century. This organization, known as the American Dog Breeders Association (ADBA), was begun by Guy McCord, a close friend of the well-known Pit Bull breeder John P. Colby. Like the UKC, the ADBA still registers the Pit Bull today.

During the 1930s, an American cinema series by the name of *Our Gang* (or *The Lil' Rascals*) featured among its regular cast of

CLUBS AND ASSOCIATIONS

Contact these organizations for more information about the Pit Bull:

United Kennel Club
100 East Kilgore Road
Kalamazoo, MI 49002-5584
(616) 343-9020
www.ukcdogs.com

American Dog Breeders Association
*exclusively for American Pit Bull Terrier breeders
Box 1771, Salt Lake City, UT 84110
members.aol.com/bstofshw/bst.html

Continental Kennel Club, Inc.
PO Box 908
Walker, LA 70785
(800) 952-3376
www.ckcusa.com

Pit Bulls were registered with the American Kennel Club as American Staffordshire Terriers by breeders who focused on conformation showing rather than working or fighting.

characters a Pit Bull by the name of "Petey," also known as "Pete the Pup." The popularity of the series and its canine mascot brought such positive attention to the breed that by 1936, the prestigious American Kennel Club (AKC) began to register the Pit Bull. Unhappy with the name of the breed, however, those responsible for registry of the breed with the AKC decided to change the breed's official name to Staffordshire Terrier and, ultimately, many years later, to American Staffordshire Terrier. During the late 1930s, then, those Pit Bulls being registered by the United Kennel Club, the American Dog Breeders Association and the American Kennel Club were all the same breed with exactly the same physical working form. Indeed breeders, such as John P. Colby, registered their dogs both as American Pit Bull Terriers with the UKC and as American Staffordshire Terriers with the AKC.

The popularity of the Pit Bull, with its various registries and with its many official breed names, waned during the 1940s and onward until roughly the mid-1970s. However, the breed was never threatened with extinction. It never reached a condition in which one could say there was no interest in these dogs at all, but other breeds became the focus of the average dog fancier's attention.

Dogs raised for fighting in America and elsewhere had their ears cropped to make them less vulnerable during combat.

During this period, those Pit Bulls registered as Staffordshire Terriers or as American Staffordshire Terriers by the AKC fell out of favor with the fighting-dog fraternity. AKC breeders focused all of their attention on competition in the show ring and left the breeding of fighting dogs to those who registered their dogs with the UKC and the ADBA.

It was during this period that a divergence in both physical type and temperament began to develop between AKC-registered dogs and the UKC- and ADBA-registered dogs. While many owners of UKC- and ADBA-registered Pit Bulls continued to breed with working form and temperament in mind, AKC breeders devoted all of their energy to producing dogs that measured up to the adopted breed standard of perfection, and therefore were best equipped to compete in the show ring. As a result, the American Staffordshire Terrier (or AmStaff) began to take on its current more blocky type, while the dogs of working lines retained their more "terrier" type.

Also during this period, the breed in both its working form and its show form, and regardless of how it was registered, enjoyed a condition of relative obscurity. It lived in peace in America. No one thought it to be a dangerous dog. Many forgot what a Pit Bull even was. Those who remembered the breed remembered it fondly from the comedy series on

television. The reputation for being dangerous was then reserved for such breeds as the Doberman Pinscher. The Pit Bull was left to its fanciers almost exclusively.

At about the time that the reputation of the Pit Bull breed began to change for the worse in the United States (about 1980), Dutch dog fighters had developed an interest in these dogs. The first Pit Bulls to find their way to Holland were serious "match dogs" acquired from hard-core American "dog men." It was not long before "underground" dog fighters in the United States began to take notice of the serious matches and breeding being conducted in Holland. From Holland, interest in the Pit Bull spread to Germany, the United Kingdom, France, Italy, parts of Scandinavia and elsewhere in Europe and throughout the world.

By the late 1980s or about 1990, the "dangerous Pit Bull" saga began to spread over the American borders to other, and even far off, countries. Following a lead established by law enforcement officials in the UK, countries began to pass laws against the ownership and importation of this breed that had been largely unknown, even in its homeland, only a few years before. An example of such legislation, this from the Nation of Singapore, appears as follows:

A BAD NAME

During the late 1970s, something unusual happened. The Pit Bull exploded in popularity, and, unfortunately, notoriety. One day, it seemed, few in America knew what a Pit Bull was, and the next day, the entire nation thought it to be the most dangerous dog in the world. Suddenly, the breed went from being a dog Americans remembered fondly to a dog everyone thought we would all be better off without. No one is quite sure why this happened. Nevertheless, the more negative talk there was about how dangerous Pit Bulls could be, in newspapers and on television reports, the more the mania spread. More and more irresponsible people wanted to own Pit Bulls; the more irresponsible owners there were, the more trouble the breed seemed to be creating.

Category A Dogs

Category A dogs are:
- Pit Bull (includes American Pit Bull Terrier, American Staffordshire Terrier, Staffordshire Bull Terrier, the American Bulldog).
- Akita.
- Neapolitan Mastiff.
- Tosa.
- Crosses of Pit Bull, Akita, Neapolitan Mastiff or Tosa.
- Category A dogs cannot be imported into Singapore as of August 1991.

Owners of Category A dogs already residing in Singapore must comply with the following conditions:
- The dog must be sterilized.
- The dog must be permanently identified with a microchip implant.
- The owner must take out a third-party insurance policy of $100,000 on the dog.
- The owner must put up a $5,000 cash bond that will be returned when the dog passes away or is no longer residing in Singapore. The bond will be forfeited if the owner allows the dog in a public place without a leash and muzzle.

Responsible people who get to know the Pit Bull value the breed for its many wonderful personality traits and abilities.

American Pit Bull Terriers can be lovable and loving family pets in the hands of the right owners.

Characteristics of the American Pit Bull Terrier

Given all that has been said, and all that one may have heard about the breed, there is no doubt that a question should have arisen in the mind of the average reader of this book. *Why the Pit Bull?* Why would any normal clear-thinking person want to own a Pit Bull? After all, we've admitted that this breed is essentially a fighting dog, haven't we? We've admitted that the breed is often dog-aggressive and that many Pit Bulls can be "people-aggressive." We've seen that many countries of the world do not allow ownership of Pit Bulls by their citizens. In some areas of the world where the Pit Bull may be legally owned, an insurance policy must be carried by the dog's owner to protect him in the event that his

HYPED UP
There are actually many sound reasons to own a little Pit Bull dog. In fact, when we remember that this breed lived among Americans for more than 100 years without anyone fearing it, we should begin to realize that the breed's currently bad reputation is more a matter of "media hype" than it is a matter of bad dogs.

neighbor is mauled!

Any breed can become the subject of the kind of breed discrimination that the Pit Bull faces today. At one time it was the Doberman Pinscher that had this reputation in the US. For a while it was the poor Saint Bernard! After all, even the Bulldog of England is a dog of pure fighting origin, but nowhere in the world is it being proposed that we outlaw Bulldogs. In time, the hysteria surrounding the Pit Bull will pass and another breed will become the focus of the media's attention. Irresponsible owners in search of an impressionable breed will turn their attention to whatever breed that will be and we will all wonder why we once

The original purpose of the American Pit Bull Terrier, as a fighting dog, has given many the wrong impression that it is unsuitable as a pet.

thought that the little Pit Bull was an inherently dangerous dog. Until that time, however, we should discuss a few of the very positive qualities of this breed.

EASY-CARE DOG

One of the first characteristics of the Pit Bull breed that many of us will find desirable is its low-maintenance body style. The Pit Bull is a short-coated dog that does not shed excessively. An occasional brushing will keep the falling hair under control and keep the carpet clean. The Pit Bull is an energetic dog when out of the home, and the breed's desire to take walks with its owner will keep its nails short and its owner, who will hopefully be on the other end of the leash, fit. Unlike the Bulldog, the Pit Bull is not a wrinkled dog and so there will be no need for regular cleaning of facial crevices.

PHYSICAL CHARACTERISTICS

The Pit Bull is not an especially large dog. In fact, in its working form, the Pit Bull is a rather small dog. This enables owners to keep a Pit Bull in a small home or apartment quite comfortably. While it is an energetic dog when given the chance to exercise, it is a breed that prefers to relax when at home. As such, it will not be in the way at all times and will not make itself more conspicuous than many owners prefer their dogs to be.

The Pit Bull also tends to be a hardy dog. It can play hard and live long without costing its owner a fortune in veterinary bills. The closer a line of Pit Bulls is to its original working stock, the hardier the dogs from that line will be. It is not the least bit unusual to own a Pit Bull for 12, 13 or 14 years, or even more. When such dogs finally succumb to old age, they tend to do it without suffering long, protracted, painful and expensive illnesses.

PERSONALITY

Above all, the Pit Bull is an incredibly devoted dog. The breed becomes highly attached to its human family and will accept no others as long as it feels welcome at home as part of that family. As an extension of this attribute, it can also be a protective dog, and a powerful and protective, yet small and convenient, dog can be very useful in the right hands with responsible ownership. However, unlike many very devoted dogs, the Pit Bull *can* accept change. Should the unfortunate situation arise when a family must give up its pet Pit Bull, the dog will become dedicated to its new owner with time. Therefore, a "second-hand" Pit Bull may be a sound option for you to consider, particularly if you are familiar with the dog's previous owners and their living situation.

Most of all, the Pit Bull is a fine companion dog. Those who know the breed will often tell you that, in their opinion, there can be no finer companion dog than the Pit Bull. It is a dog that will bond to its entire human family, but one that will always hold a special place in its heart for the person it decides is its closest friend. It is a dog that will always

> ### DEVELOPING POTENTIAL
> The behavior and personality of your Pit Bull will reflect your care and training more than any breed characteristics or indications. Remember that these dogs require a purposeful existence and plan your relationship around activities that serve this most basic and important need. All of the good potential of the breed will naturally follow.

be there for its owner. It is a forgiving breed, an exceedingly loyal breed, a fun-loving breed and a lifelong friend.

VERSATILITY OF THE BREED
We have accepted unabashedly the fact that the Pit Bull as a breed is the most adept "game dog" ever to have been produced. We also know of the Pit Bull's utilization as a "catch dog."

Guard work and personal protection work are other areas in which the Pit Bull breed often excels. The Pit Bull generally makes a useful home guardian and personal protection dog, primarily because it is such a devoted and determined breed. It is not a dog that automatically protects whatever space it happens to be occupying or whatever person happens to be holding its leash. Instead, it is a breed that will often defend due to a sense of devotion to its family and its family's property.

Who says American Pit Bull Terriers aren't lovable, gentle pets?

CATCH DOGS

The work of the catch dog is to run down, seize and hold free-range animals, such as free-range hogs, on large farms and ranches. The dog should be agile, powerful, fearless and determined enough to hold the free-range animal until the farmer or rancher can tie it. This kind of work often requires greater physical size than many Pit Bulls possess, but Pit Bulls on the upper end of the size scale, in the 65-pound and over range, serve very well as catch dogs.

THE BEST HOME FOR A PIT BULL

Before getting into the question of where to get your pup, we should consider the question of what types of homes are most appropriate for the Pit Bull breed. It is all too common these days for authors of breed books to present their breed as being ideal for every home. This is not true in any case and neither is it true in the case of the Pit Bull.

The Pit Bull is an ideal dog for an adult family with older (14 years and above) children and

The Pit Bull is an ideal pet for families with children over 14 years of age. The whole family should take part in the Pit Bull's training and care from the very beginning.

A beautiful, alert, intelligent American Pit Bull Terrier in healthy, muscular condition.

with someone at home most of the time. The size of the home is not as important—it can be large, with a fenced yard, or small. It can even be an apartment in the city. The important thing is that someone is often home and someone is willing to take the dogs on regular long walks. This describes the best of all possible situations for the Pit Bull.

Conversely, the worst situation for a Pit Bull is one in which a dog is raised by a young person who, when the dog is older, becomes too busy to spend much time with the dog. Worse still is that this young person has children when the dog is grown and these children end up spending

time with a dog that doesn't relate to them as true "members of the family." This is how so many of the disasters we read about in the tabloids happen.

Not too long ago, a story erupted in all of the local newspapers in a particular American town. The story told of a Pit Bull that had killed and seriously mutilated the body of the young child it was living with "for no apparent reason." The dog immediately was euthanized by the local authorities and the community began calling for a total ban on the ownership of Pit Bulls in the city.

The dog was examined to confirm its breed, and, unfortunately, it was without question a Pit Bull. But the authorities were questioned about the circumstances of the killing, and the details are as follows. You decide who or what is to blame for the child's death.

A young unmarried woman who lived alone in an urban area had a baby. The father of the baby lived in an apartment of his own with his male Pit Bull. The man was a drug dealer. The dog was six years old and had never lived with anyone but this man. The dog had been fully and professionally attack-trained at a young age and occasional refresher lessons had been provided throughout its life.

When the woman's baby was three months old, the father decided to move in with her and the child. She was so happy that the baby's father would be moving in that she decided they should go out and celebrate. They had no babysitter for the three-month-old child, but the man assured the mother of the baby that the dog could be trusted to protect the home and its juvenile occupant in their absence. Besides, he said, they would only be out for a few hours.

The man brought the dog to the woman's home, where the dog met the infant for the first time. It was locked in the apartment with the infant and the couple left the two alone. Neigh-

bors said that within half an hour of the time that the couple left the apartment, the infant began to cry out loud. Shortly after that, the crying stopped and growling was heard. The infant was never seen alive again and the dog was put down the next day. The owner of the dog swore that the dog had never acted in such an unpredictable, irrational manner before. After all, the dog had lived with him, and if anyone was in a position to evaluate the temperament of the dog, that someone would have to be him. Furthermore, he said, the dog had been trained!

Would any breed of dog be appropriate for the situation I just described? Was that particular dog to blame for having murdered a child? Should the Pit Bull breed be held responsible in a situation like this? Is this breed a problem or does this breed currently suffer from the problem of irresponsible, and indeed downright stupid, ownership? Well, this is now for you to decide.

In any event, this was possibly the absolute worst environment for any Pit Bull to find itself living in. Again, the absolute best environment for the Pit Bull is with an adult family with grown children. Another fine situation for a Pit Bull is an adult couple with no children or a retired adult in need of some serious companionship.

Pit Bull owners often engage their dogs in games that utilize the dog's agility and strong jaws.

OWNER SUITABILITY

Being the perfect Pit Bull owner involves understanding your dog and complying with certain breed demands, but it also involves selecting this breed because it fits into your own lifestyle. For example, if you own another dog and you know that your dogs will be unattended for a few hours each day, the Pit Bull may simply be the wrong breed for you. After all, fighting between your Pit Bull and other dogs you may meet on the street is easily discouraged. However, leaving two dogs alone for hours at a time, on a regular basis, with one of the two being a

Pit Bull, may be too much to ask of this breed. We must understand that when all is said and done, the Pit Bull is a fighting dog.

If you are a working person or half of a working couple, and you desire a pet that you can leave alone all day, almost every day, a dog of any breed is really the wrong pet for you. There will be other times in your life for a dog, but this would seem not to be the right time.

Even if you are a person who simply hates to take a walk on a regular basis, the Pit Bull will be the wrong breed for you. There are other breeds that can live in such an environment. You would be doing both yourself and the Pit Bull breed a favor if you would select one of those breeds instead.

The perfect owner for a Pit Bull Terrier is one who will return the devotion the dog will provide him. This owner will want the dog primarily for the fantastic companionship it will afford and not for the image it will exude. This owner will enjoy the exercise the breed demands as much as his dog itself will. This owner will understand the reputation by which the breed has become victimized and work to improve it. This owner will be in a position to take on a dog that may be with him for 15 years, without expecting the dog to deal with excessive change in its life. This owner will be one who can

THE WRONG OWNER

The Pit Bull breed is not high on the list of dogs to be recommended for a family expecting children or for a situation in which the dog will be left alone for extended periods of time on a regular basis. Other than that, this is a fine family dog.

For example, if you are a young man who knows that within a few years you will be married and maybe have a child, this would be the wrong time to buy yourself a Pit Bull pup. This is an unfortunately common mistake. Too many young people make the decision to obtain a Pit Bull pup with the full knowledge that within a few years their lifestyles will be completely different than it is when they acquire the dog.

provide a very regular routine in all respects.

If you are this person, the Pit Bull may be a better choice from among pure-bred dogs than you may formerly have thought.

HIP DYSPLASIA IN PIT BULLS

The Pit Bull is a generally healthy breed and the closer a dog is to working stock, the healthier it will be. One situation that deserves special mention here is the condition of hip dysplasia as it relates to the working Pit Bull. While there is no doubt that this is a serious condition for many breeds, and selecting a pup should generally include questions about the condition of the breeding stock's hips, in some situations this concern can become overdone. In the case of the working-stock Pit Bull, overemphasized concern is often the case.

Shortly after the United Kennel Club became very involved in showing their registered Pit Bulls in conformation shows, show Pit Bull breeders began having their breeding stock tested for hip dysplasia. An alarm was sounded throughout the United States because the vast majority of the Pit Bulls being tested were found to be very dysplastic. None of these dysplastic dogs showed any outward evidence of suffering from this condition, and all of the breeding stock from which these dogs had been produced had been hard-

working, long-lived, super-athletic
fighting dogs!

There is a difference between
what we can think of as "actual"
dysplasia and "theoretical"
dysplasia. If you will be selecting
your pup from proven, highly
game-bred, long-lived working
stock, questions about medical
evidence that the hips are tightly
formed are not as imperative as
they might be in other, especially
larger, breeds.

VARIATIONS IN THE BREED
Earlier, we began to discuss the
first divergence in type between
the Pit Bull in its working form,
as represented by dogs registered
with the United Kennel Club and
the American Dog Breeders Association, and the breed in its show
form, as represented by dogs
registered as American Staffordshire Terriers with the American

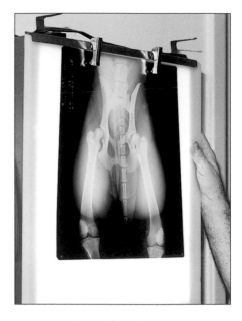

Kennel Club. This divergence in
type is common among breeds
that are registered by show organizations but that remain in use
in the field elsewhere, such as
sporting breeds like the Labrador
Retriever and English Setter.
Rarely are successful show dogs
also successful field or "working"
dogs, especially in the US, where
working ability does not affect a
dog's earning a championship. In
the UK, on the other hand, the
working and gundog breeds, for
example, must qualify in the
field before they can be considered full champions.

In the case of the Pit Bull,
the situation has become even
more complicated in recent
years. Today we see at least three
forms of the Pit Bull breed; these

There is a large divergence in type among the Pit Bull breed—those that make the best working dogs would often not be successful in the show ring.

three forms can be labeled as the working (fighting) form, the show form and the "backyard-bred" form.

Working-form Pit Bulls, also referred to as the game-bred type, tend to be smaller, finer boned, more terrier-type dogs. Temperamentally, these dogs tend to be aggressive toward other dogs, but not toward people. In fact, years ago, the game-bred Pit Bull had the reputation of being one of the most useless of breeds for protection work because they were so reluctant to display aggression toward people.

Show-form Pit Bulls tend to be larger, more refined, bigger boned dogs with greater, more expansive chests and larger heads. Temperamentally, these dogs tend to be less dog-aggressive and not very aggressive toward people.

The "backyard-bred" dog tends to be larger than the working dog. It is not a refined-looking animal. It is not bred to last in long sustained dog matches and it is not bred to win any shows. It is

Acquire your pet American Pit Bull from stock that has been bred for temperament rather than fighting ability. Investigate the background of the parents and the breeder.

generally bred to be attractive to those seeking a very macho-looking dog. Temperamentally, these dogs tend to be more aggressive toward people and often more outwardly aggressive toward other animals as well. After all, those who want a macho-looking dog are generally also in the market for a dog that will threaten others. Those who see a market in selling Pit Bulls to these people tend to selectively breed for this quality.

In selecting a Pit Bull for your own home, it is perhaps more important than with any other breed to do your homework carefully. The game-bred dog might not be the poor choice for a pet that you thought it to be. The show dog is often a fine pet. But the backyard-bred dog is what has given rise to the "Pit Bull problems" and negative reputation we have seen in recent years.

Some lines of Pit Bull produce dogs that are noticeably stockier and larger than dogs of other lines.

According to the standard, it is not important whether the dog's ears are cropped or uncropped. Uncropped ears give the Pit Bull a softer look.

Breed Standard for the American Pit Bull Terrier

WHAT IS A BREED STANDARD?

Every breed of dog is guided by a standard, a blueprint of sorts that describes the breed's physical properties and temperament, and the traits necessary for the task for which the dog originally was bred. Although Pit Bulls today are seen as pets, in the show ring and as guard dogs rather than in their original capacity as fighting dogs, the physical characteristics that made the dogs able fighters are what define the breed's type, and these qualities of strength and athleticism should not be lost in today's breed representatives. Standards are written by knowl-

The upper teeth should meet outside and in front of the lower teeth, in what is known as a scissors bite. Strong teeth and jaws are hallmarks of the breed.

edgeable breed experts who hope to ensure the quality of their given breed for future generations. Breeders follow the standard when planning a mating, and show judges use the standard to evaluate dogs in the ring. Without such guidelines, specific inherent breed characteristics may be altered or completely eliminated. The following breed standard is that of the United Kennel Club, the first organization to recognize and register the American Pit Bull Terrier.

A head study of a dog with cropped ears.

THE UNITED KENNEL CLUB STANDARD FOR THE AMERICAN PIT BULL TERRIER

Head: Medium length. Bricklike in shape. Skull flat and widest at

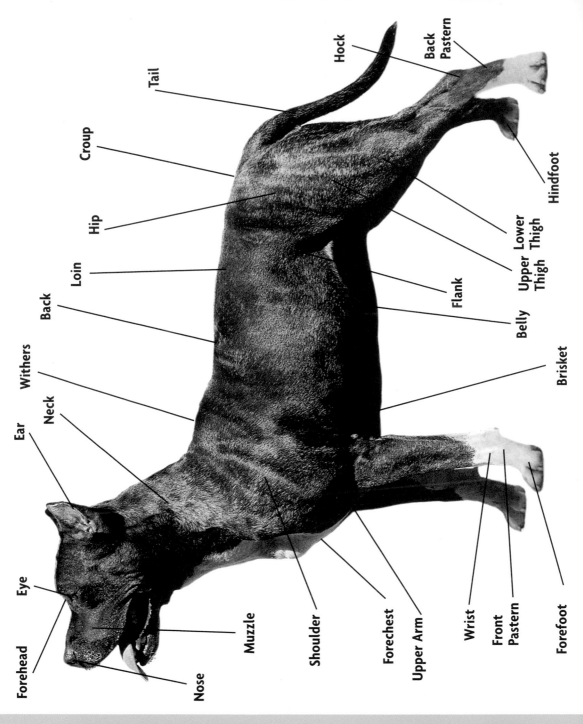

Tail

Hock

Back Pastern

Croup

Hindfoot

Hip

Lower Thigh

Upper Thigh

Loin

Flank

Back

Belly

Withers

Brisket

Neck

Ear

Eye

Forehead

Muzzle

Nose

Shoulder

Forechest

Upper Arm

Wrist

Front Pastern

Forefoot

PHYSICAL STRUCTURE OF THE AMERICAN PIT BULL TERRIER

This dog exhibits attractive brindle coloration and a head of desirable shape. You can see how wide and flat the head is between the ears.

the ears, with prominent cheeks free from wrinkles.

Muzzle: Square, wide and deep. Well-pronounced jaws, displaying strength. Upper teeth should meet tightly over lower teeth, outside in front.

Ears: Cropped or uncropped (not important). Should be set high on head, and be free from wrinkles.

Eyes: Round. Should be set far apart, low down on the skull. Any color acceptable.

Nose: Wide-open nostrils. Any color acceptable.

Neck: Muscular. Slightly arched. Tapering from shoulder to head. Free from loose skin.

Shoulders: Strong and muscular, with wide sloping shoulder blades.

Back: Short and strong. Slightly sloping from withers to rump. Slightly arched at loins, which should be slightly tucked.

Chest: Deep, but not too broad, with wide sprung ribs.

BREEDING CONSIDERATIONS

The decision to breed your dog is one that must be considered carefully and researched thoroughly before moving into action. Some people believe that breeding will make their bitches happier or that it is an easy way to make money. Unfortunately, indiscriminate breeding only worsens the rampant problem of pet overpopulation, as well as putting a considerable dent in your pocketbook. As for the bitch, the entire process from mating through whelping is not an easy one and puts your pet under considerable stress. Last, but not least, consider whether or not you have the means to care for an entire litter of pups. Without a reputation in the field, your attempts to sell the pups may be unsuccessful.

The Pit Bull's body should convey an overall impression of strength, power and athleticism.

Ribs: Close. Well sprung, with deep back ribs.

Tail: Short in comparison to size. Set low and tapering to a fine point. Not carried over back. Bobbed tail not acceptable.

Legs: Large, round boned, with straight, upright pasterns, reasonably strong. Feet to be of medium size. Gait should be light and springy. No rolling or pacing.

Thigh: Long with muscles developed. Hocks down and straight.

Coat: Glossy. Short and stiff to the touch.

Color: Any color or markings are permissible.

Weight: Not important. Females preferred from 30 to 50 pounds. Males from 35 to 60 pounds.

Scale of Points
General appearance, personality and obedience: 20
Head, muzzle, eyes and ears: 25
Neck, shoulders and chest: 15
Body: 15
Legs and feet: 15
Tail, coat and color: 10
Total: 100

Any color or marking is acceptable according to the standard. This dog's glistening jet-black coat color is an attractive variety.

Selecting an American Pit Bull puppy is a serious task. You must choose a properly bred pup from a responsible breeder who concentrates on sound temperament.

Your Puppy
American Pit Bull Terrier

CHOOSING YOUR BREEDER AND PUPPY

Choosing a Pit Bull pup for a family pet will involve an even more serious approach than in the case of many other breeds. It is necessary to find a pup that will mature to be the kind of dog that will be appropriate for your family. We must keep in mind that at this especially sensitive time in the existence of the Pit Bull breed, the reputation of the breed is really in question in the minds of many who will meet your dog. A poorly bred dog or a poorly socialized puppy will make a negative impression upon those who will meet your dog, and the last thing this breed needs is for people to get further negative impressions.

Avoid buying a puppy from any breeder who appears to have no goal in his breeding program. If a breeder's goal is to breed "highly protective" (man-aggressive) Pit Bulls, avoid that breeder. A well-chosen Pit Bull will become devoted to you. A devoted dog will protect you, should the need to do so arise. You don't need a Pit Bull from outwardly aggressive stock. You don't need a dog that displays aggression unnecessarily. Such a

INHERIT THE MIND
In order to know whether or not a puppy will fit into your lifestyle, you need to assess his personality. A good way to do this is to interact with his parents. Your pup inherits not only his appearance but also his personality and temperament from the sire and dam. If the parents are fearful or overly aggressive, these same traits may likely show up in your puppy.

dog will only scare your neighbors, becoming a serious liability for you and adding fuel to the fire begun by those who would outlaw this breed worldwide.

A pup from steady show stock can be a good choice. Outward aggression is often discouraged among show breeders, as there is no place for such aggression in the show ring. I do feel I need to warn you that winning conformation shows is not what this breed is all about, however. When the characteristics for which a breed was originally produced are totally ignored in a breeding program, a breed changes. Just as there are some undesirable qualities in the "backyard-bred dog," many of the truly positive and most definitive qualities of the game-bred dog can also be lost in a genetic line. Nonetheless, for most prospective owners, the highly show-bred dog is probably the best choice for pups.

COMMITMENT OF OWNERSHIP
After considering all of these factors, you have most likely already made some very important decisions about selecting your puppy. You have chosen the Pit Bull, which means that you have decided that the breed's characteristics are what you want in a dog and that the Pit Bull will fit well into your family and lifestyle. If you have selected a breeder, you have gone a step further—you have done your research and found a responsible, conscientious person who breeds quality Pit Bulls and who should be a reliable source of help as you and your puppy adjust to life together. If you have observed a

litter in action, you have obtained a firsthand look at the dynamics of a puppy "pack" and, thus, you have gotten to learn about each pup's individual personality—perhaps you have even found one that particularly appeals to you.

However, even if you have not yet found the Pit Bull puppy of your dreams, observing pups will help you learn to recognize certain behavior and to determine what a pup's behavior indicates about his temperament. You will be able to pick out which pups are the leaders, which ones are less outgoing, which ones are confident, which ones are shy, playful, friendly,

GAME-BRED
With a word of caution, I will not advise the prospective owner to avoid bringing home a pup from a truly game-bred litter. This is the real Pit Bull, after all. All of the qualities that originally endeared so many Pit Bull owners of the past to this breed are most commonly expressed in the game-bred dog. The Pit Bull is a dog of unlimited devotion to its human masters, as the Pit Bull match scenario shamefully proves. At no point in a serious Pit Bull match is any human participant afraid to enter the pit. A dog can be furious. It can be intent upon destroying its opponent. It can be exhausted. Indeed, it can be dying of its wounds. But it does not take its aggression out on its handler. How many other breeds can we say this about?

aggressive, etc. Equally as important, you will learn to recognize what a healthy pup should look and act like. All of these things will help you in your search, and when you find the Pit Bull that was meant for you, you will know it!

Researching your breed, selecting a responsible breeder and observing as many pups as possible are all necessary steps on the way to dog ownership. It may seem like a lot of effort…and you have not even brought the pup home yet! Remember, though, you cannot be too careful when it comes to deciding on the type of dog you want and finding out about your prospective pup's background. Buying a puppy is not—or should not be—just another whimsical purchase. In fact, this is one instance in which you actually *do* get to choose your own family! But, you may be thinking, buying a puppy should be fun—it should not be so serious and so much work. If you keep in mind the thought that your puppy is not a cuddly stuffed toy or decorative lawn ornament, but instead will become a real member of your family, you will realize that while buying a puppy is a pleasurable and exciting endeavor, it is not something to be taken lightly. Relax…the fun will start when the pup comes home!

Always keep in mind that a puppy is nothing more than a baby in a furry disguise…a baby who is

American Pit Bulls are great jumpers with strong jaws. They can easily support their own weight when they grasp a suspended object.

virtually helpless in a human world and who trusts his owner for fulfillment of his basic needs for survival. That goes beyond food, water and shelter; your pup needs care, protection, guidance and love. If you are not prepared to commit to this, then you are not prepared to own a dog.

"Wait a minute," you say. "How hard could this be? All of my

BOY OR GIRL?

An important consideration is the sex of your puppy. For a family companion, a bitch may be the better choice, considering the female's inbred concern for all young creatures and her accompanying tolerance and patience. Pet dogs that will not be bred or shown should be neutered (males) or spayed (females), as it could guarantee them longer lives.

"YOU BETTER SHOP AROUND!"

Finding a reputable breeder who sells healthy pups is very important, but make sure that the breeder you choose is not only someone you respect but also someone with whom you feel comfortable. Your breeder will be a resource long after you buy your puppy, and you must be able to call with reasonable questions without being made to feel like a pest! If you don't connect on a personal level, investigate some other breeders before making a final decision.

Bull pup to be a well-adjusted and well-mannered adult dog—a dog that could be your most loyal friend.

PREPARING PUPPY'S PLACE IN YOUR HOME

Researching your breed and finding a breeder are only two aspects of the homework you will have to do before bringing your Pit Bull puppy home. You will also have to prepare your home and family for the new addition. Much like you would prepare a nursery for a newborn baby, you will need to

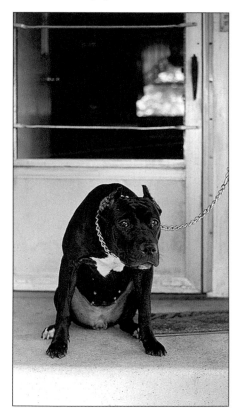

neighbors own dogs and they seem to be doing just fine. Why should I have to worry about all of this?" Well, you *should not* worry about it; in fact, you will probably find that once your Pit Bull pup gets used to his new home, he will fall into his place in the family quite naturally. But it never hurts to emphasize the commitment of dog ownership. With some time and patience, it is really not too difficult to raise a curious and exuberant Pit

Pit Bulls make very effective guard dogs just by their looks alone!

Playful nipping may seem cute in a pup, but discourage it early on. You will not want to contend with this behavior in a full-grown Pit Bull.

designate a place in your home that will be the puppy's own. How you prepare your home will depend on how much freedom the dog will be allowed: will he be confined to one room or a specific area in the house, or will he be allowed to roam as he pleases? Will he spend most of his time in the house or will he be primarily an outdoor dog? Whatever you decide, you must ensure that he has a place that he can "call his own."

When you bring your new puppy into your home, you are bringing him into what will become his home as well. Obviously, you did not buy a puppy so that he could take control and "rule the roost," but in order for a puppy to grow into a stable, well-adjusted

dog, he has to feel comfortable in his surroundings. Remember, he is leaving the warmth and security of his mother and littermates, plus the familiarity of the only place he has ever known, so it is important to make his transition as easy as possible. By preparing a place in your home for the puppy, you are making him feel as welcome as possible in a strange new place. It should not take him long to get used to it, but the sudden shock of being transplanted is somewhat traumatic for a young pup. Imagine how a small child would feel in the same situation—that is how your puppy must be feeling. It is up to you to reassure him and to let him know, "Little fellow, you are going to like it here!"

WHAT YOU SHOULD BUY

CRATE

To someone unfamiliar with the use of crates in dog training, it may seem like punishment to shut a dog in a crate; this is not the case at all. Crates are not cruel—crates have many humane and highly effective uses in dog care and training. For example, crate training is a very popular and very successful house-breaking method; a crate can keep your dog safe during travel; and, perhaps most importantly, a crate provides your dog with a place of his own in your home. It serves as a "doggie bedroom" of sorts—your Pit Bull can curl up in his crate when he wants to sleep or when he just needs a break. Many dogs sleep in their crates overnight. When lined with soft bedding and with his favorite toy inside, a crate becomes a cozy pseudo-den for your dog. Like his ancestors, he too will seek out the comfort and retreat of a den—you just happen to be providing him with something a little more luxurious than leaves and twigs lining a dirty ditch.

As far as purchasing a crate, the type that you buy is up to you. It will most likely be one of the two most popular types: wire or fiber-glass. There are advantages and disadvantages to each type. For example, a wire crate is more open, allowing the air to flow through and affording the dog a view of what is going on around him. Wire crates are the best choice for use in the home. A fiberglass crate, however, is recommended for use as a travel crate since it provides more protection for the dog.

The size of the crate is another thing to consider. Puppies do not stay puppies forever—in fact, some-times it seems as if they grow right before your eyes. A small crate may be fine for a very young Pit Bull pup, but it will not do him much good for long! Unless you have the money and the inclination to buy a new crate every time your pup has a growth spurt, it is better to get one that will accommodate your dog both as a pup and at full size. A medium to large crate will be necessary for a full-grown Pit Bull. With much size variation in the

breed, the line from which your pup comes will help you predict his eventual size.

BEDDING

A blanket or crate pad in the dog's crate will help the dog feel more at home. First, the bedding will take the place of the leaves, twigs, etc., that the pup would use in the wild to make a den; the pup can make his own "burrow" in the crate. Although your pup is far removed from his den-making ancestors, the denning instinct is still a part of his genetic makeup. Second, until you bring your pup home, he has been sleeping amid the warmth of his mother and littermates, and while a blanket is not the same as a warm, breathing body, it will still provide heat and something with which to snuggle. You will want to wash your pup's bedding frequently in

case he has an accident in his crate, and replace or remove any bedding that becomes ragged and starts to fall apart.

TOYS

Toys are a must for dogs of all ages, especially for curious playful pups. Puppies are the "children" of the dog world, and what child does not love toys? Chew toys provide enjoyment to both dog and owner—your dog will enjoy playing with his favorite toys, while you will enjoy the fact that they distract him from chewing on your expensive shoes and leather sofa.

Obtain a large crate for your Pit Bull. Puppies grow; crates don't!

CRATE-TRAINING TIPS

During crate training, you should partition off the section of the crate in which the pup stays. If he is given too big an area, this will hinder your training efforts. Crate training is based on the fact that a dog does not like to soil his sleeping quarters, so it is ineffective to keep a pup in an area that is so big that he can eliminate in one end and get far enough away from it to sleep. Also, you want to make the crate den-like for the pup. Blankets and a favorite toy will make the crate cozy for the small pup; as he grows, you may want to evict some of his "roommates" to make more room. It will take some coaxing at first, but be patient. Given some time to get used to it, your pup will adapt to his new home-within-a-home quite nicely.

Always supervise your pup's explorations—a curious pup can get himself into trouble!

Puppies love to chew; in fact, chewing is a physical need for pups as they are teething, and everything looks appetizing! The full range of your possessions—from old dish rag to Oriental rug—are fair game in the eyes of a teething pup. Puppies are not all that discerning when it comes to finding something to literally "sink their teeth into"—everything tastes great!

Pit Bull puppies and adults are aggressive chewers. They have strong teeth and jaws, even as youngsters. Only the hardest, strongest toys should be offered to them; look for "indestructible" toys designed for strong-jawed dogs, increasing the size of the toys as the Pit Bull grows up. Be careful of stuffed toys, as a pup can de-stuff one pretty quickly, and stay away from stuffed toys with small plastic

Puppies love to play and love to chew, so it's no surprise that most anything looks like a chew toy!

TOYS, TOYS, TOYS!

With a big variety of dog toys available, and so many that look like they would be a lot of fun for a dog, be careful in your selection. It is amazing what a set of puppy teeth can do to an innocent-looking toy; so, obviously, safety is a major consideration. Be sure to choose the most durable products that you can find. This is an especially important consideration with a breed like the Pit Bull, who has naturally strong teeth and jaws. Hard nylon bones and toys are a safe bet, and many of them are offered in different scents and flavors that will be sure to capture your dog's attention. It is always fun to play a game of fetch with your dog, and there are balls and flying discs that are specially made to withstand dog teeth.

eyes or parts that a pup could choke on. Similarly, squeaky toys are quite popular, but these are not advised for free play. Supervise your dog with these types of toys or do not offer them at all. Again, if a pup chews apart one of these, the small plastic squeaker inside can be

dangerous if swallowed. Monitor the condition of your pup's toys carefully and get rid of any that have been chewed to the point of becoming potentially dangerous.

Also be careful of natural bones, which have a tendency to splinter into sharp, dangerous pieces. A Pit Bull will have no problem breaking up a natural bone, and this could be very harmful to him. Also be careful of rawhide, which after enough chewing can turn into pieces that are easy to swallow, and watch out for the mushy mess it can turn into on your carpet.

Leash

A nylon leash is probably the best option, as it is the most resistant to puppy teeth should your pup take a liking to chewing on his leash. Of course, this is a habit that should be nipped in the bud, but if your pup likes to chew on his leash he has little chance of being

A proper leash is a necessity. It must be sturdy and comfortable both for you to handle and for the dog to wear.

able to chew through the strong nylon. Nylon leashes are also lightweight, which is good for a young Pit Bull who is just getting used to the idea of walking on a leash. For everyday walking and safety purposes, the nylon leash is a good choice for a Pit Bull pup. However, because of the breed's natural strength, you should purchase a stronger leash for your adult Pit Bull, especially if he tends to pull on the leash while walking. Some Pit Bull owners favor using harnesses to take their dogs for walks, so the choice is up to you—whatever works best for you and your Pit Bull.

Collar

Your pup should get used to wearing a collar all the time since you will want to attach his ID tags to his collar. Also, the leash and collar go hand in hand—you have to

Provide your puppy with safe chew toys to encourage proper chewing and avoid destructive behavior.

attach the leash to something! A lightweight nylon collar will be a good choice; make sure that it fits snugly enough so that the pup cannot wriggle out of it, but loose enough so that it will not be uncomfortably tight around the pup's neck. You should be able to fit a finger in between the pup and the collar. It may take some time for your pup to get used to wearing the collar, but soon he will not even notice that it is there. Choke collars are made for training, but a choke collar should only be used by an owner who knows exactly how to use it. If you use a stronger leather leash or a chain leash to walk your Pit Bull, you will need a stronger collar as well. There are specialty items made with strong, muscular breeds like the Pit Bull in mind. As such, you will often see Pit Bulls wearing very thick, perhaps studded, leather collars.

This Pit Bull wears a studded collar for looks only and has his leash attached to another strong, thick collar.

ARE YOU PREPARED?

Unfortunately, when a puppy is bought by someone who does not take into consideration the time and attention that dog ownership requires, it is the puppy who suffers when he is either abandoned or placed in a shelter by a frustrated owner. So all of the "homework" you do in preparation for your pup's arrival will benefit you both. The more informed you are, the more you will know what to expect and the better equipped you will be to handle the ups and downs of raising a puppy. Hopefully, everyone in the household is willing to do his part in raising and caring for the pup. The anticipation of owning a dog often brings a lot of promises from excited family members: "I will walk him every day," "I will feed him," "I will house-train him," etc., but these things take time and effort, and promises can easily be forgotten once the novelty of the new pet has worn off.

FOOD AND WATER BOWLS

Your pup will need two bowls, one for food and one for water. You may want two sets of bowls, one for inside and one for outside, depending on where the dog will be fed and where he will be spending most of his time. Stainless steel or sturdy plastic bowls are popular choices. Although plastic bowls are more chewable, dogs tend not to chew on the steel variety, which can also be sterilized. It is advised to put your Pit Bull's food and water bowls on specially made elevated stands; this brings the food closer to the dog's level so he does not have to crane his neck to eat, thus aiding his digestion and helping to guard against bloat or gastric torsion. It is important to buy sturdy bowls since, again, anything is in danger of being chewed by puppy teeth and you do not want your Pit Bull to be constantly chewing apart his bowl (for his safety and for your wallet!).

FEEDING TIPS

You will probably start feeding your pup the same food that he has been getting from the breeder; the breeder should give you a few days' supply to start you off. Although you should not give your pup too many treats, you will want to have puppy treats on hand for coaxing, training, rewards, etc. Be careful, though, as a small pup's calorie requirements are relatively low and a few treats can add up to almost a full day's worth of calories without the required nutrition.

CLEANING SUPPLIES

A pup that is not housebroken means you will be doing a lot of cleaning until he is. "Accidents" will occur, which is okay for now because he does not know any better. All you can do is clean up any accidents—old rags, paper towels, newspapers and a safe disinfectant are good to have on hand.

Your puppy will require only a lightweight collar. Accustom him to wearing it at a young age.

BEYOND THE BASICS

The items previously discussed are the bare necessities. You will find out what else you need as you go along—grooming supplies, flea/tick protection, baby gates to partition a room, etc.—these things will vary depending on your situation. It is just important that right away you have everything you need to feed and make your Pit Bull comfortable in his first few days at home.

PUPPY-PROOFING YOUR HOME

Aside from making sure that your Pit Bull will be comfortable in your home, you also have to make sure that your home is safe for your Pit Bull. This means taking precautions to make sure that your pup will not get into anything he should not get into and that there is nothing within his reach that may harm him should he sniff it, chew it, inspect it, etc. This probably seems obvious since, while you are primarily concerned with your pup's safety, at the same time you do not want your belongings to be ruined. Breakables should be

placed out of reach if your dog is to have full run of the house. If he is to be limited to certain places within the house, keep any potentially dangerous items in the "off-limits" areas. An electrical cord can pose a danger should the puppy decide to taste it—and who is going to convince a pup that it would not make a great chew toy? Cords should be fastened tightly against the wall and kept from puppy teeth. If your dog is going to spend time in a crate, make sure that there is nothing near his crate that he can reach if he sticks his curious little nose or paws through the openings. And just as you would with a child, keep all household cleaners and chemicals (antifreeze is especially dangerous to dogs) where the pup cannot get to them.

OUTDOOR SAFETY

It is just as important to make sure that the outside of your home is safe. Of course, your puppy should never be unsupervised, but a pup let loose in the yard will want to run and explore, and he should be granted that freedom. Do not let a fence give you a false sense of security; you would be surprised how crafty (and persistent) a Pit Bull can be in figuring out how to dig under and squeeze his way through small holes, or to jump or climb over a fence. The remedy is to make the fence high enough so that it really is impossible for your dog to get over it (about 6 feet should suffice), and well embedded into the ground. Many Pit Bulls are very good climbers, though, so always keep an eye open. Be sure to repair or secure any gaps in the fence. Check the fence periodically to ensure that it is in good shape and make repairs as needed; a very determined pup may return to the same spot to "work on it" until he is able to get through.

FIRST TRIP TO THE VET

Okay, you have picked out your puppy, your home and family are ready—now all you have to do is pick your Pit Bull up from the breeder and the fun begins, right?

Well...not so fast. Something else you need to prepare for is your pup's first trip to the veterinarian. Perhaps the breeder can recommend someone in the area who specializes in Pit Bulls, or maybe you know some other Pit Bull owners who can suggest a good vet. Either way, you should have an appointment arranged for your pup before you pick him up; plan on taking him for a check-up within the first few days of bringing him home.

The pup's first visit will consist of an overall examination to make sure that the pup does not have any problems that are not apparent to you. The veterinarian will also set up a schedule for the pup's vaccinations; the breeder will inform you of which ones the pup has already received and the vet can continue from there.

INTRODUCTION TO THE FAMILY

Everyone in the house will be excited about the puppy's coming home and will want to pet him and play with him, but it is best to make the introduction low-key so as not to overwhelm the puppy. He is apprehensive already; it is the first time he has been separated from his mother and the breeder, and the ride to your home is likely the first time he has been in a car. The last thing you want to do is smother him, as this will only frighten him further. This is not to say that human contact is not

HEALTH GUARANTEE
Your breeder may have offered a health guarantee. If not, do not feel awkward about asking for one as part of your sales agreement. An honest and reputable breeder will not be insulted. A health guarantee states that the breeder will take the pup back and give the buyer a refund if the vet discovers a problem. A health guarantee may also cover any hereditary diseases that show up before a certain age, in which case the breeder would provide a replacement. The exact terms will differ depending on what is discussed and put in writing between the breeder and the buyer, but make sure that you are in accord with the terms before you agree to purchase the pup and that you read all paperwork carefully.

extremely necessary at this stage, because this is the time when an instant connection between the pup and his human family are formed. Gentle petting and soothing words should help console him, as well as just putting him down and letting him explore on his own (under your watchful eye, of course).

The pup may approach the family members or may busy himself with exploring for a while. Gradually, each person should spend some time with the pup, one at a time, crouching down to get as close to the pup's level as possible, letting him sniff each person's

Pit Bulls love to be near their owners and aren't shy about showing it.

hands and petting him gently. He definitely needs human attention and he needs to be touched—this is how to form an immediate bond. Just remember that the pup is experiencing a lot of things for the first time, all at the same time. There are new people, new noises, new smells and new things to investigate, so be gentle, be affectionate and be as comforting as you can be.

YOUR PUP'S FIRST NIGHT HOME

You have traveled home with your new charge safely in his crate. He's been to the vet for a thorough checkup; he's been weighed, his papers examined; perhaps he's even been vaccinated and wormed as well. He's met the family and licked the whole family, including the excited children and the less-than-happy cat. He's explored his area, his new bed, the yard and anywhere else he's been permitted. He's eaten his first meal at home and relieved himself in the proper place. He's heard lots of new sounds, smelled new friends and seen more of the outside world than ever before.

That was the just the first day! He's exhausted and is ready for bed…or so you think!

It's puppy's first night and you are ready to say "Good night"— keep in mind that this is puppy's first night ever to be sleeping alone. His dam and littermates are no longer at paw's length and he's a bit scared, cold and lonely. Be reassuring to your new family member, but this is not the time to spoil him and give in to his inevitable whining.

Many breeders recommend placing a piece of bedding from his former home in his new bed so that he recognizes the scent of his littermates. Others still advise placing a hot water bottle in his bed for warmth. This latter may be a good idea provided the pup doesn't attempt to suckle—he'll get good and wet and may not fall asleep so fast.

BEDTIME

Puppies whine. They whine to let the others know where they are and hopefully to get company out of it. At bedtime, place your pup in his new bed or crate in his room and close the crate door. Mercifully, he will fall asleep without a peep. If the inevitable occurs, ignore the whining; he is fine. Be strong and keep his interest in mind. Do not allow your heart to become guilty and visit the pup. He will fall asleep.

Puppy's first night can be somewhat stressful for the pup and his new family. Remember that you are setting the tone of nighttime at your house. Unless you want to play with your pup every night at 10 p.m., midnight and 2 a.m., don't initiate the habit. Surely your family will thank you, and eventually so will your pup!

PREVENTING PUPPY PROBLEMS

SOCIALIZATION

Now that you have done all of the preparatory work and have helped your pup get accustomed to his new home and family, it is about time for you to have some fun! Socializing your Pit Bull pup gives you the opportunity to show off your new friend, and your pup gets to reap the benefits of being an adorable small creature that people will adore, want to pet and, in general, think is absolutely precious! Introducing your Pit Bull to the neighbors and letting them see what a friendly dog he is will do wonders for their perception of the breed.

Your Pit Bull puppy should be exposed to other people, animals and situations. This will help him become well adjusted as he grows up and less prone to being timid or fearful of the new things he will encounter. Your pup's socialization began at the breeder's; now it is your responsibility to continue. The socialization he receives up until

Puppies love to explore and can wind up in unexpected places if not carefully supervised.

the age of 12 weeks is the most critical, as this is the time when he forms his impressions of the outside world. Lack of socialization can manifest itself in fear and aggression as the dog grows up. He needs lots of human contact, affection, handling and exposure to other animals. Be careful during the eight-to-ten-week-old period, also known as the fear period. The interaction he receives during this time should be especially gentle and reassuring.

Once your pup has received his necessary vaccinations, feel free to take him out and about (on his leash, of course). Take him around the neighborhood, take him on your daily errands, let people pet him, let him meet other dogs and pets, etc. Puppies do not have to try to make friends; there will be no shortage of people who will want to introduce themselves. Just make sure that you carefully supervise each meeting. If

> ## QUALITY FOOD
> The cost of food must be mentioned. This is not a breed that can be maintained on table scraps and light supplement. Pit Bulls need a good supply of protein to develop the bone and muscle required in a working animal. Pit Bulls are not picky eaters but, unless fed properly, can quickly succumb to skin problems.

Rope toys are recommended, but tug-of-war games are not.

the neighborhood children want to say hello, for example, that is great—children and pups most often make great companions. But sometimes an excited child can unintentionally handle a pup too roughly, or an overzealous pup can playfully nip a little too hard. You want to make socialization experiences positive ones and give a favorable impression of the breed. What a pup learns during this very formative stage will impact his attitude toward future encounters. A pup that has a bad experience with a child may grow up to be a dog that is shy around or aggressive toward children, and you want your dog to be comfortable around everyone.

Consistency in Training
Dogs, being pack animals, naturally need a leader, or else they try to establish dominance in their packs. When you bring a dog into your family, who becomes the leader and who becomes the "pack" are entirely up to you! Your pup's intu-

itive quest for dominance, coupled with the fact that it is nearly impossible to look at an adorable Pit Bull pup, with his "puppy-dog" face and his endlessly wagging tail, and not cave in, give the pup almost an unfair advantage in getting the upper hand! And a pup will definitely test the waters to see what he can and cannot get away with. Do not give in to those pleading eyes—stand your ground when it comes to disciplining the pup and make sure that all family members do the same. It will only confuse the pup when Mother tells him to get off the couch when he is used to sitting up there with Father to watch the nightly news. Avoid discrepancies by having all members of the household decide on the rules before the pup even comes home…and be consistent in enforcing them! Early training

shapes the dog's personality, so you cannot be unclear in what you expect.

COMMON PUPPY PROBLEMS

The best way to prevent problems is to be proactive in stopping an undesirable behavior as soon as it starts. The old saying "You can't teach an old dog new tricks" does not necessarily hold true, but it *is* true that it is much easier to discourage bad behavior in a young developing pup than to wait until the pup's bad behavior becomes the adult dog's bad habit. There are some problems that are especially prevalent in puppies as they develop.

NIPPING

As puppies start to teethe, they feel the need to sink their teeth into anything…unfortunately that includes your fingers, arms, hair, toes…whatever happens to be available. You may find this behavior cute for about the first five seconds…until you feel just how sharp those puppy teeth are. This is something you want to discourage immediately and consistently with a firm "No!" (or whatever number of firm "Nos" it takes for him to understand that you mean busi-

CHEWING TIPS

Chewing goes hand in hand with nipping in the sense that a teething puppy is always looking for a way to soothe his aching gums. In this case, instead of chewing on you, he may have taken a liking to your favorite shoe or something else which he should not be chewing. Again, realize that this is a normal canine behavior that does not need to be discouraged, only redirected. Your pup just needs to be taught what is acceptable to chew on and what is off-limits. Consistently tell him "No!" when you catch him chewing on something forbidden and give him a chew toy.

Conversely, praise him when you catch him chewing on something appropriate. In this way, you are discouraging the inappropriate behavior and reinforcing the desired behavior. The puppy's chewing should stop after his adult teeth have come in, but an adult dog continues to chew for various reasons—perhaps because he is bored, needs to relieve tension or just likes to chew. That is why it is important to redirect his chewing when he is still young.

Dogs must be trained at a young age not to jump up and beg at the table.

Puppies cry and whine for attention, especially when they are left alone. The trick is to comfort the puppy without coddling him.

ness) and replace your finger with an appropriate chew toy. While this behavior is merely annoying when the dog is still young, it can become dangerous as your Pit Bull's adult teeth grow in and his jaws develop. You do not want a Pit Bull to grow up thinking that it's okay to nip at humans, as this can lead to biting, and the breed's jaws are very strong. The pup does not mean any harm with a friendly nip, but he also does not know his own strength.

CRYING/WHINING

Your pup will often cry, whine, whimper, howl or make some type of commotion when he is left alone. This is basically his way of calling out for attention, of calling out to make sure that you know he is there and that you have not forgotten about him. He feels insecure when he is left alone; for example, when you are out of the house and he is in his crate or when you are in another part of the house and he cannot see you. The noise he is making is an expression of the anxiety he feels at being alone, so he needs to be taught that being alone is okay. You are not actually training the dog to stop making noise, you are training him to feel comfortable when he is alone and thus removing the need for him to make the noise. This is where the crate with cozy bedding and a favorite toy comes in handy. You want to know that he is safe

when you are not there to supervise, and you know that he will be safe in his crate rather than roaming freely about the house. In order for the pup to stay in his crate without making a fuss, he needs to be comfortable in his crate. On that note, it is extremely important that the crate is never used as a form of punishment, or the pup will have a negative association with the crate.

Accustom the pup to the crate in short, gradually increasing time intervals in which you put him in the crate, maybe with a treat, and stay in the room with him. If he cries or makes a fuss, do not go to him, but stay in his sight. Gradually he will realize that staying in his crate is okay without your help, and it will not be so traumatic for him when you are not around. You may want to leave the radio on softly when you leave the house; the sound of human voices may be comforting to him.

POISONOUS PLANTS

Below is a partial list of plants that are considered poisonous. These plants can cause skin irritation, illness and even death. You should be aware of the types of plants that grow in your yard and garden and that you keep in your home. Special care should be taken to rid your home of dangerous plants indoors and out, and to keep all plants in the household out of your Pit Bull's reach.

American Blue Flag	Japanese Yew
Bachelor's Button	Jerusalem Cherry
Barberry	Jimson Weed
Bog Iris	Lily of the Valley
Boxwood	Marigold
Buttercup	Milkwort
Cherry Pits	Mistletoe (berries)
Chinese Arbor	Monkshood
Chokecherry	Mullein
Climbing Lily	Narcissus
Crown of Thorns	Peony
Elderberry (berries)	Persian Ivy
Elephant Ear	Rhododendron
English Ivy	Rhubarb
False Acacia	Shallon
Fern	Siberian Iris
Foxglove	Solomon's Seal
Hellebore	Star of Bethlehem
Herb of Grace	Water Lily
Holly	Wood Spurge
Horse Chestnut	Wisteria
Iris (bulb)	Yew

Everyday Care of Your American Pit Bull Terrier

DIETARY AND FEEDING CONSIDERATIONS

You have probably heard it a thousand times, you are what you eat. Believe it or not, it's very true. For dogs, they are what you feed them because they don't make their own choices about what they eat. Even those people who truly want to feed their dogs the best often don't know how to do so because they do not know which foods are best for their dogs.

Dog foods are produced in three basic types: dry, semi-moist and canned. Dry foods are for the cost-conscious because they are much less expensive than semi-moist and canned foods. Dry foods contain the least fat and the most preservatives. Most canned foods are 60–70% water, while semi-moist foods are so full of sugar that they are the least preferred by owners, though dogs welcome them.

Three stages of development must be considered when selecting a diet for your dog: the puppy stage, the adult stage and the senior stage.

PUPPY STAGE

Puppies have a natural instinct to suck milk from their mother's breasts. They should exhibit this behavior the first day of their lives. If they don't suckle within a few hours, the breeder should attempt to put them onto their mother's nipples. Their failure to feed means that the breeder will have to feed them himself under the advice and guidance of a veterinarian. This will involve a baby bottle and a special formula. Despite there being some excellent formulas available, their mother's milk is the best because it contains colostrum, a sort of antibiotic milk which protects the puppy during the first eight to ten weeks of their lives.

Puppies should be allowed to nurse for about six weeks and they should be slowly weaned

You are advised to follow the instructions of the breeder in feeding your new Pit Bull puppy.

away from their mother by introducing small portions of meat or moist food after they are about one month old.

By the time they are eight weeks old, they should be completely weaned and fed solely a puppy food. During this weaning period, their diet is most important, as a puppy grows fastest during his first year of life. Growth foods can be recommended by your veterinarian and the puppy should be kept on this diet for about 18 months, depending on the individual dog's development.

Puppy diets should be balanced for your dog's needs and supplements of vitamins, minerals and protein should not be necessary.

ADULT DIETS

A dog is considered an adult when he has stopped growing. The growth is in height and/or length. Do not consider the dog's weight when the decision is made to switch from a puppy diet to an adult-maintenance diet. Again you should rely upon your veterinarian to recommend an acceptable maintenance diet. Major dog-food manufacturers specialize in this type of food and it is just necessary for you to select the one best suited to your dog's needs. For example, active dogs will have different requirements than sedate dogs.

FOOD PREFERENCE

Selecting the best dry dog food is difficult. There is no majority consensus among veterinary scientists as to the value of nutrient analysis (protein, fat, fiber, moisture, ash, cholesterol, minerals, etc.). All agree that feeding trials are what matter most, but you also have to consider the individual dog. The dog's weight, age and activity level, and what pleases his taste, all must be considered. It is probably best to take the advice of your veterinarian. Every dog's dietary requirements vary, even during the lifetime of a particular dog.

If your dog is fed a good dry food, it does not require supplements of meat or vegetables. Dogs do appreciate a little variety in their diets, so you may choose to stay with the same brand but vary the flavor. Alternatively, you may wish to add a little flavored stock to give a difference to the taste.

Pups get the best start in life by nursing from their mother and receiving the essential protective qualities of colostrum.

A Pit Bull reaches adulthood at about two years of age, though some dogs fully mature at 16 months, while others may take up to three years, which is why each dog is an individual in terms of changing the diet.

SENIOR DIETS

As dogs get older, their metabolism changes. The older dog usually exercises less, moves more slowly and sleeps more. This change in lifestyle and physiological performance requires a change in diet. Since these changes take place slowly, they might not be recognizable. What is easily recognizable is weight gain. By continually feeding your dog an adult-maintenance diet when he is slowing down metabolically, your dog will gain weight. Obesity in an older dog compounds the health problems that already accompany old age.

As your dog gets older, few of his organs function up to par. The kidneys slow down and the intestines become less efficient. These age-related factors are best handled with a change in diet and a change in feeding schedule to give smaller portions that are more easily digested.

There is no single best diet for every older dog. While many dogs do well on light or senior diets, other dogs do better on other special premium diets such as lamb and rice. Be sensitive to

DRINK, DRANK, DRUNK— MAKE IT A DOUBLE

In both humans and dogs, as well as other living organisms, water forms the major part of nearly every body tissue. Naturally, we take water for granted, but without it, life as we know it would cease.

For dogs, water is needed to keep their bodies functioning biochemically. Additionally, water is needed to replace the water lost while panting. Unlike humans, who are able to sweat to dissipate heat, dogs must pant to cool down, thereby losing the vital water from their bodies need to regulate their body temperatures. Humans lose electrolyte-containing products and other body-fluid components through sweating; dogs do not lose anything except water.

Water is essential always, but especially so when the weather is hot or humid or when your dog is exercising or working vigorously.

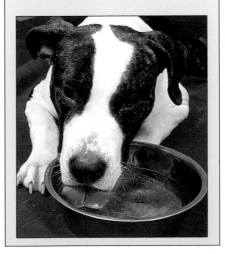

your senior Pit Bull's diet and this will help control other problems that may arise with your old friend.

WATER

Just as your dog needs proper nutrition from his food, water is an essential "nutrient" as well. Water keeps the dog's body properly hydrated and promotes normal function of the body's systems. During housebreaking, it is necessary to keep an eye on how much water your Pit Bull is drinking, but once he is reliably trained he should have access to clean fresh water at all times. Make sure that the dog's water bowl is clean, and change the water often.

EXERCISE

All dogs require some form of exercise, regardless of breed. A sedentary lifestyle is as harmful to a dog as it is to a person. The

"What can we do today?" The versatile and athletic Pit Bull is always up for a new type of exercise or activity with his owner.

Pit Bull happens to be an active and naturally muscular breed, but he does not need excessively strenuous workouts to keep his body in good shape. The Pit Bull seems to develop and maintain muscle quite easily, but not without some sort of activity. Regular walks, play sessions in the yard or letting the dog run free in the fenced yard under your supervision are all sufficient forms of exercise for the Pit Bull. For those who are more ambitious, you will find that your adult Pit Bull will be able to keep up with you on extra-long walks or your morning run. Real enthusiasts may want to try weight pulling with their Pit Bulls, but that requires more time, practice and equipment.

Not only is exercise essential to keep the dog's body fit, it is also essential to his mental well-being. A bored dog will find something to do, which often manifests itself in some type of destructive behavior. In this sense, it is essential for the owner's mental well-being as well!

GROOMING

BRUSHING

A natural bristle brush or a slicker brush can be used for routine brushing. Daily brushing is effective for stimulating the dog's natural oils to add shine and a healthy look to the coat. Your Pit

Bull is not a breed that needs excessive grooming; in fact, he is rather low-maintenance. However, his short, close-lying, sleek coat needs to be brushed as part of routine maintenance. Daily brushing will help rid the coat of dust and dandruff and will remove any dead hair. Pit Bulls do shed, but no special attention is necessary during shedding times if you are diligent about your routine brushing. Basically, the goal in grooming your Pit Bull is to keep his skin and coat healthy and to keep him looking good. Regular grooming sessions are also a good way to spend time with your dog. Many dogs grow to like the feel of being brushed and will enjoy the daily routine.

BATHING

Dogs do not need to be bathed as often as humans, but bathing as needed is important for healthy skin and a clean, shiny coat. Again, like most anything, if you accustom your pup to being bathed as a puppy, it will be second nature by the time he grows up. You want your dog to be at ease in the bath or else it could end up a wet, soapy, messy ordeal for both of you!

Brush your Pit Bull to remove any dead hair and debris before wetting his coat. Make sure that your dog has a good non-slip surface to stand on. Begin by wetting the dog's coat. A shower

GROOMING EQUIPMENT
How much grooming equipment you purchase will depend on how much grooming you are going to do. Here are some basics:
• Natural bristle brush
• Slicker brush
• Metal comb
• Scissors
• Rubber mat
• Dog shampoo
• Spray hose attachment
• Heavy towels
• Blow dryer
• Ear cleaner
• Cotton balls
• Nail clippers

or hose attachment is necessary for thoroughly wetting and rinsing the coat. Check the water temperature to make sure that it is neither too hot nor too cold.

Next, apply shampoo to the dog's coat and work it into a good lather. You should purchase a shampoo that is made for dogs; do not use a product made for human hair. Wash the head last; you do not want shampoo to drip into the dog's eyes while you are washing the rest of his body. Work the shampoo all the way down to the skin. You can use this opportunity to check the skin for any bumps, bites or other abnormalities. Do not neglect any area of the body—get all of the hard-to-reach places.

SOAP IT UP

The use of human soap products like shampoo, bubble bath and hand soap can be damaging to a dog's coat and skin. Human products are too strong; they remove the protective oils coating the dog's hair and skin that make him water-resistant.

The only time a Pit Bull needs a bath is when he gets a dirty coat or when the vet prescribes a medicated bath. In any case, only use shampoo made especially for dogs.

Once the dog has been thoroughly shampooed, he requires an equally thorough rinsing. Shampoo left in the coat can be irritating to the skin. Protect his eyes from the shampoo by shielding them with your hand and directing the flow of water in the opposite direction. You should also avoid getting water in the ear canal. Be prepared for your dog to shake the excess water out of his coat—you might want to stand back, but make sure you have a hold on the wet dog to keep him from running through the house.

EAR CLEANING

The ears should be kept clean and any excess hair inside the ear should be trimmed. Ears can be cleaned with a cotton ball and special cleaner or ear powder made for dogs. Be on the lookout for any signs of infection or ear-mite infestation. If your Pit Bull has been shaking his head or scratching at his ears frequently, this usually indicates a problem. If his ears have an unusual odor, this is a sure sign of mite infestation or infection, and a signal to have his ears checked by the vet.

NAIL CLIPPING

Your Pit Bull should be accustomed to having his nails trimmed at an early age, since it will be a part of your maintenance routine throughout his life. Not only does it look nicer, but a dog with long nails can cause injury if he jumps up or if he scratches someone unintentionally. Also, a long nail has a better chance of ripping and bleeding, or causing the feet to spread. A good rule of thumb is that if you can hear your dog's nails' clicking on the floor when he walks, his nails are too long.

Cleaning your dog's ears is a necessary part of grooming. Use a cotton ball and clean gently, never entering the ear canal.

Clipping your Pit Bull's nails is important. Start when he is a puppy so he will become accustomed to his routine pedicures.

Before you start cutting, make sure you can identify the "quick" in each nail. The quick is a blood vessel that runs through the center of each nail and grows close to the end. It will bleed if cut, which will be quite painful for the dog as it contains nerve endings. Keep some type of clotting agent on hand, such as a styptic pencil or styptic powder (the type used for shaving). This will stop the bleeding quickly when applied to the end of the cut nail. Do not panic if this happens, just stop the bleeding and talk soothingly to your dog. Once he has calmed down, move on to the next nail. It is better to clip a little at a time, particularly with black-nailed dogs.

Hold your pup steady as you begin trimming his nails; you do not want him to make any sudden movements or run away. Talk to him soothingly and stroke his fur as you clip. Holding his foot in your hand, simply take off the end of each nail in one quick clip. You can purchase nail clippers that are specially made for dogs; you can probably find them wherever you buy grooming supplies.

TRAVELING WITH YOUR DOG

CAR TRAVEL
You should accustom your Pit Bull to riding in the car at an early age. You may or may not often take him in the car, but at

> **TRAVEL TIP**
> Never leave your dog alone in the car. In hot weather, your dog can die from the high temperature inside a closed vehicle; even a car parked in the shade can heat up very quickly. Leaving the window open is dangerous as well since the dog can hurt himself trying to get out.

the very least he will need to go to the vet and you do not want these trips to be traumatic for the dog or a big hassle for you. The safest way for a dog to ride in the car is in his crate. If he uses a fiberglass crate in the house, you can use the same crate for travel. If you have a wire crate in the house, consider purchasing an appropriately sized fiberglass or wooden crate for traveling. Wire crates can be used for car travel, but fiberglass or wooden crates are sturdier and safer.

Put the pup in the crate and see how he reacts. If he seems uneasy, you can have a passenger hold him on his lap while you drive. Another option is a specially made safety harness for dogs, which straps the dog in much like a seat belt. Do not let the dog roam loose in the vehicle— this is *very* dangerous! If you should stop short, your dog can be thrown and injured. If the dog starts climbing on you and pestering you while you are driving, you will not be able to concentrate on the road. It is an unsafe situation for everyone—human and canine.

For long trips, be prepared to stop to let the dog relieve himself. Bring along whatever you need to clean up after him. You should bring along some old towels and rag, in case he has an accident in the car or becomes carsick.

AIR TRAVEL

Contact your chosen airline before proceeding with your travel plans that include your Pit Bull. Exact policies and procedures regarding traveling with and transporting pets vary from airline to airline, and some airlines have imposed an embargo on Pit Bulls, meaning that they do not allow the breed on the airline. Some airlines also do not allow pets to travel as checked baggage during the summer months to avoid heat-related complications.

If you are able to transport your Pit Bull, the dog will be required to travel in a fiberglass crate and you should always check in advance with the airline regarding specific requirements for the crate's size, type and labeling, as the crate must fall within these guidelines. To help put the dog at ease, give him one of his favorite toys in the crate. Do not feed the dog for several hours prior to checking in so that you minimize his need to relieve himself. However, some airlines

require that the dog must be fed within a certain time of arriving at the airport, in which case a light meal is best. For long trips, you will have to attach food and water bowls to the dog's crate so that airline employees can tend to him between legs of the trip. Again, as each airline's specifics on things such as food, crate type, health certificates, international travel, etc., vary, you must be sure that you have acquainted yourself well ahead of time with the regulations of the airline on which you are traveling.

Make sure your dog is properly identified and that your contact information appears on his ID tags and on his crate. Your Pit Bull will travel in a different area of the plane than the human passengers, so every rule must be strictly followed to prevent the risk of getting separated from your dog.

VACATIONS AND BOARDING

So you want to take a family vacation—and you want to include *all* members of the family.

Dog licenses as well as ID tags with your name, address and telephone number should be attached to your dog's collar, which he must always wear.

Tattooing is a popular form of identification. This dog is tattooed on the inside of her rear leg, where the tattoo is easily visible.

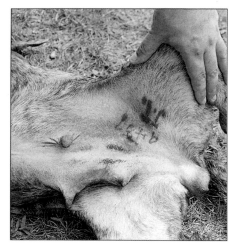

You would probably make arrangements for accommodations ahead of time anyway, but this is especially important when traveling with a dog. You do not want to make an overnight stop at the only place around for miles to find out that they do not allow dogs. Also, you do not want to reserve a place for your family without mentioning that you are bringing a dog, because, if it is against their policy, you may not have a place to stay.

Alternatively, if you are traveling and choose not to bring your Pit Bull, you will have to make arrangements for him while you are away. Some options are to have the dog stay with a neighbor whom he knows well, to have a trusted familiar friend stop by often or stay at your house or to bring your dog to a reputable boarding kennel. If you choose to board him at a kennel, you should stop by to see the facility and where the dogs are kept to make sure that it is clean. Talk to some of the employees and see how they treat the dogs—do they spend time with the dogs, play with them, supervise them, exercise them, etc.? You know that your Pit Bull will not be happy unless he gets regular activity. Also find out the kennel's policy on vaccinations and what they require. This is for all of the dogs' safety, since when dogs are kept together, there is a greater risk of diseases being passed from dog to dog. Kennel cough, also known as tracheobronchitis, is a prime concern. Many veterinarians offer boarding facilities; this is another option.

IDENTIFICATION
Your Pit Bull is your valued companion and friend. That is why you always keep a close eye on him and you have made sure that he cannot escape from the yard or wriggle out of his collar and run away from you. However, accidents can happen and there may come a time when your dog unexpectedly gets separated from you. If this unfortunate event should occur, the first thing on your mind will be finding him. Proper identification in the form of an ID collar, a tattoo or microchip will increase the chances of his being returned to you safely and quickly.

Training Your American Pit Bull Terrier

Living with an untrained dog is a lot like owning a piano that you do not know how to play—it is a nice object to look at, but it does not do much more than that to bring you pleasure. Now try taking piano lessons, and suddenly the piano comes alive and brings forth magical sounds and rhythms that set your heart singing and your body swaying.

The same is true with your Pit Bull. At first you enjoy seeing him around the house. He does not do much with you other than to need food, water and exercise. Come to think of it, he does not bring you much joy, either. He is a big responsibility with a very small return. And often, he develops unacceptable behaviors that annoy you, to say nothing of bad habits that may end up costing you great sums of money. Not a good thing!

Now train your Pit Bull. Enroll in an obedience class. Teach him good manners as you learn how and why he behaves the way he does. Find out how to communicate with your dog and how to recognize and understand his communications with you. Suddenly the dog takes on a new role in your life—he is smart, interesting, well behaved and fun to be with, and he demonstrates his bond of devotion to you daily. In other words, your Pit Bull does wonders for your ego because he constantly reminds you that you

REAP THE REWARDS

If you start with a normal, healthy dog and give him time, patience and some carefully executed lessons, you will reap the rewards of that training for the life of the dog. And what a life it will be! The two of you will find immeasurable pleasure in the companionship you have built together with love, respect and understanding.

are not only his leader, you are his hero! Miraculous things have happened—you have a wonderful dog (even your family and friends have noticed the transformation!) and you feel good about yourself.

Those involved with teaching dog obedience and counseling owners about their dogs' behavior have discovered some interesting facts about dog ownership. For example, training dogs when they are puppies results in the highest rate of success in developing well-mannered and well-adjusted adult dogs. Training an older dog, say from six months to six years of age, can produce almost equal results, providing that the owner accepts the dog's slower rate of learning capability and is willing to work patiently to help the dog succeed at developing to his fullest potential. Unfortunately, the patience factor is what many owners of untrained adult dogs lack, so they do not persist until their dogs are successful at learning particular behaviors.

Training a puppy, for example, aged 8 to 16 weeks (20 weeks at the most), is like working with a dry sponge in a pool of water. The pup soaks up whatever you show him and constantly looks for more things to do and learn. At this early age, his body is not yet producing hormones, and

Despite the "macho" image, the trained Pit Bull is a friendly and gentle pet.

These dogs, having been let out to relieve themselves, are waiting to be allowed back into the house. This behavior is learned during the housebreaking process.

therein lies the reason for such a high rate of success. Without hormones, he is focused on his owners and not particularly interested in investigating other places, dogs, people, etc. You are his leader: his provider of food, water, shelter and security. Therefore, he latches onto you and wants to stay close. He will usually follow you from room to room, will not let you out of his sight when you are outdoors with him and will respond in like manner to the people and animals you encounter. If, for example, you greet a friend warmly, he will be happy to greet the person as well. If, however, you are hesitant or anxious about the approach of a stranger, he will respond accordingly.

Once the puppy begins to produce hormones, his natural curiosity emerges and he begins to investigate the world around him. It is at that time when you may

FAMILY TIES

If you have other pets in the home and/or interact often with the pets of friends and other family members, your pup will respond to those pets in much the same manner as you do. It is only when you show fear of or resentment toward another animal that he will act fearful or unfriendly.

notice that the untrained dog begins to wander away from you and even ignore your commands to stay close. When this behavior becomes a problem, the owner has two choices: get rid of the dog or train him. It is strongly urged that you choose the latter option.

Occasionally there are no classes available within a reasonable distance from the owner's home. Sometimes there are classes available but the tuition is too costly. Whatever the circumstances, the solution to training your Pit Bull without formal lessons lies within the pages of this book.

This chapter is devoted to helping you train your Pit Bull at

It is best to train your Pit Bull as a puppy, when he is most receptive to learning.

> **HIS OWN LITTLE CORNER**
> Mealtime should be a peaceful time for your puppy. Do not put his food and water bowls in a high-traffic area in the house. For example, give him his own little corner of the kitchen where he can eat undisturbed and where he will not be underfoot. Do not allow small children or other family members to disturb the pup when he is eating.

home. If the recommended procedures are followed faithfully, you may expect positive results that will prove rewarding to both you and your dog.

Whether your Pit Bull is a puppy or a mature adult, the methods of teaching and the techniques we use in training basic behaviors are the same. After all, no dog, whether puppy or adult, likes harsh or inhumane methods. All creatures, however, respond favorably to gentle motivational methods and sincere praise and encouragement. Now let us get started.

HOUSEBREAKING

You can train a puppy to relieve himself wherever you choose. For example, city dwellers often train their puppies to relieve themselves on the sidewalk because large plots of grass are not readily available. Of course, they must always carry plastic bags or "poop-scoops" to clean up after

Canine Development Schedule

It is important to understand how and at what age a puppy develops into adulthood. If you are a puppy owner, consult the following Canine Development Schedule to determine the stage of development your American Pit Bull Terrier puppy is currently experiencing. This knowledge will help you as you work with the puppy in the weeks and months ahead.

Period	Age	Characteristics
FIRST TO THIRD	BIRTH TO SEVEN WEEKS	Puppy needs food, sleep and warmth, and responds to simple and gentle touching. Needs mother for security and disciplining. Needs littermates for learning and interacting with other dogs. Pup learns to function within a pack and learns pack order of dominance. Begin socializing with adults and children for short periods. Pup begins to become aware of his environment.
FOURTH	EIGHT TO TWELVE WEEKS	Brain is fully developed. Needs socializing with outside world. Remove from mother and littermates. Needs to change from canine pack to human pack. Human dominance necessary. Fear period occurs between 8 and 16 weeks. Avoid fright and pain.
FIFTH	THIRTEEN TO SIXTEEN WEEKS	Training and formal obedience should begin. Less association with other dogs, more with people, places, situations. Period will pass easily if you remember this is pup's change-to-adolescence time. Be firm and fair. Flight instinct prominent. Permissiveness and over-disciplining can do permanent damage. Praise for good behavior.
JUVENILE	FOUR TO EIGHT MONTHS	Another fear period about 7 to 8 months of age. It passes quickly, but be cautious of fright and pain. Sexual maturity reached. Dominant traits established. Dog should understand sit, down, come and stay by now.

NOTE: THESE ARE APPROXIMATE TIME FRAMES. ALLOW FOR INDIVIDUAL DIFFERENCES IN PUPPIES.

their dogs. Suburbanites, on the other hand, usually have yards to accommodate their dogs' needs.

Outdoor training includes such surfaces as grass, dirt and cement. Indoor training usually means training your dog to newspaper, but this is not a viable option with a dog the size of the Pit Bull. When deciding on the surface and location that you will want your Pit Bull to use, be sure it is going to be permanent. Training your dog to grass and then changing your mind two months later is extremely difficult for both dog and owner.

Next, choose the command you will use each and every time you want your puppy to void. "Hurry up" and "Let's go" are examples of commands commonly used by dog owners.

Get in the habit of asking the puppy, "Do you want to go out?" (or whatever your chosen relief command is) before you take him out. That way, when he becomes an adult, you will be able to determine if he wants to go out when you ask him. A confirmation will be signs of interest such

Dogs are able to identify their relief areas just by sniffing.

THE SUCCESS METHOD
Success that comes by luck is usually short-lived. Success that comes by well-thought-out proven methods is often more easily achieved and permanent. The author's Success Method is designed to give you, the puppy owner, a simple yet proven way to help your puppy develop clean living habits and a feeling of security in his new environment.

as wagging his tail, watching you intently, going to the door, etc.

PUPPY'S NEEDS
Your puppy will need to relieve himself after play periods, after each meal, after he has been sleeping and any time he indicates that he is looking for a place to urinate or defecate. The urinary and intestinal tract muscles of very young puppies are not fully developed. Therefore, like human babies, puppies need to relieve themselves frequently. Take your puppy out often—every hour for an eight-week-old, for example. The older the puppy, the less often he will need to relieve himself. Finally, as a mature healthy adult, he will require only three to five relief trips per day.

HOUSING
Since the types of housing and control you provide for your puppy have a direct relationship on the success of housebreaking,

we consider the various aspects of both before we begin training.

Bringing a new puppy home and turning him loose in your house can be compared to turning a child loose in a sports arena and telling the child that the place is all his! The sheer enormity of the place would be too much for him to handle.

Instead, offer the puppy clearly defined areas where he can play, sleep, eat and live. A room of the house where the family gathers is the most obvious choice. Puppies are social animals and need to feel a part of the pack right from the start. Hearing your voice, watching you while you are doing things and smelling you nearby are all positive reinforcers that he is now a member of your pack. Usually a family room, the kitchen or a nearby adjoining breakfast area is ideal for providing safety and security for both puppy and owner.

Within that room, there should be a smaller area that the puppy can call his own. A wire or fiberglass dog crate or a partitioned-off (not boarded!) corner from which he can view the activities of his new family will be fine. The size of the area or crate is the key factor here. It must be large enough for the puppy to lie down and stretch out as well as stand up without rubbing his head on the top, yet

HOUSE-TRAINING TIP
Most of all, be consistent. Always take your dog to the same location, always use the same command and always have the dog on leash when he is in his relief area, unless a fenced-in yard is available.

By following the method described herein, your puppy will be completely housebroken by the time his muscle and brain development reach maturity. Keep in mind that small breeds usually mature faster than large breeds, but all puppies should be trained by six months of age.

small enough so that he cannot relieve himself at one end and sleep at the other without coming into contact with his droppings during the housebreaking process.

The crate or area should be lined with a clean towel and offer one toy, no more. Do not put food or water in the crate before housebreaking has been achieved, as eating and drinking will activate the pup's digestive processes and ultimately defeat your purpose as well as make the puppy very uncomfortable as he attempts to "hold it."

Dogs are, by nature, clean animals and will not remain close to their relief areas unless forced to do so. In those cases, they then become dirty dogs and usually remain that way for life.

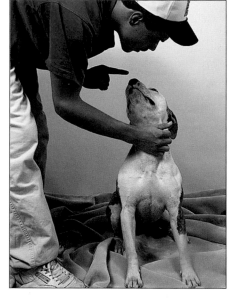

Don't waste your time in chastizing your dog if you don't catch him in the act. He'll never know the reason for his being disciplined!

THE CLEAN LIFE
By providing sleeping and resting quarters that fit the dog, and offering frequent opportunities to relieve himself outside his quarters, the puppy quickly learns that the outdoors is the place to go when he needs to urinate or defecate. It also reinforces his innate desire to keep his sleeping quarters clean. This, in turn, helps develop the muscle control that will eventually produce a dog with clean living habits.

CONTROL

By *control*, we mean helping the puppy to create a lifestyle pattern that will be compatible to that of his human pack (*you!*). Just as we guide little children to learn our way of life, we must show the puppy when it is time to play, eat, sleep, exercise and even entertain himself.

Your puppy should always sleep in his crate. He should also learn that, during times of household confusion and excessive human activity such as at breakfast when family members are preparing for the day, he can play by himself in relative safety and comfort in his crate. Each time you leave the puppy alone, he should be crated. Puppies are chewers. They cannot tell the difference between what is safe to chew on and lamp cords, television wires, shoes, table legs, etc. Chewing into a television wire, for example, can be fatal to the puppy, while a shorted wire can start a fire in the house.

If the puppy chews on the arm of the chair when he is alone, you will probably discipline him angrily when you get home. Thus, he makes the association that your coming home means he is going to be punished. (He will not remember chewing up the chair and is incapable of making the association of the discipline with his naughty deed.)

Times of excitement, such as family parties, friends' visits, etc., can be fun for the puppy, providing he can view the activities from the security of his crate. He is not underfoot and he is not being fed all sorts of tidbits that will probably cause him stomach distress, yet he still feels a part of the fun.

> **PAPER CAPER**
> Never line your pup's sleeping area with newspaper. Puppy litters are usually raised on newspaper and, once in your home, the puppy will immediately associate newspaper with voiding. Never put newspaper on any floor while house-training, as this will only confuse the puppy. Finally, restrict water intake after evening meals. Offer a few licks at a time—never let a young puppy (or an adult dog, for that matter) gulp water after meals.

SCHEDULE

As stated earlier, a puppy should be taken to his relief area each time he is released from his crate, after meals, after play sessions, when he first awakens in the morning (at age eight weeks, this can mean 5 a.m.!) and whenever he indicates by circling or sniffing busily that he needs to urinate or defecate. For a puppy less than ten weeks of age, a routine of taking him out every hour is necessary. As the puppy grows, he will be able to wait for longer periods of time.

Keep trips to his relief area short. Stay no more than five or six minutes and then return to the house. If he goes during that time, praise him lavishly and take him indoors immediately. If he does not, but he has an accident when you go back indoors, pick him up immediately, say "No! No!" and

When you take your dog to his relief area, keep the time as short as possible to encourage him to do his business quickly.

By the time the dog matures, he should be completely house-broken and trained in the basic commands.

return to his relief area. Wait a few minutes, then return to the house again. *Never* hit a puppy or put his face in urine or excrement when he has an accident!

Once indoors, put the puppy in his crate until you have had time to clean up his accident. Then release him to the family area and watch him more closely than before. Chances are, his accident was a result of your not picking up his signal or waiting too long before offering him the opportunity to relieve himself. *Never* hold a grudge against the puppy for accidents.

Let the puppy learn that going outdoors means it is time to relieve himself, not play. Once trained, he will be able to play indoors and out and still differentiate between the times for play versus the times for relief.

Help the pup develop regular

hours for naps, being alone, playing by himself and just resting, all in his crate. Encourage him to entertain himself while you are busy with your activities. Let him learn that having you near is comforting, but it is not your main purpose in life to provide him with your undivided attention.

Each time you put a puppy in his crate, tell him "Crate time!" (or whatever command you choose). Soon, he will run to his crate when he hears you say those words.

In the beginning of his training, do not leave him in his crate for prolonged periods of time except during the night when everyone is sleeping. Make his experience with his crate a pleasant one and, as an adult, he will love his crate and willingly stay in it for several hours. There are

PLAN TO PLAY

The puppy should also have regular play and exercise sessions when he is with you or a family member. Exercise for a very young puppy can consist of a short walk around the house or yard. Playing can include fetching games with a large ball or a special toy. (All puppies teethe and need soft things upon which to chew.) Remember to restrict play periods to indoors within his living area (the family room, for example) until he is completely house-trained.

millions of people who go to work every day and leave their adult dogs crated while they are out of the house. The dogs accept this as their lifestyle and look forward to "crate time."

Crate training provides safety for you, the puppy and the home. It also provides the puppy with a feeling of security, and that helps the puppy achieve self-confidence and clean habits.

Remember that one of the primary ingredients in house-training your puppy is control. Regardless of your lifestyle, there will always be occasions when you will need to have a place where your dog can stay and be happy and safe. Crate training is the answer for now and in the future.

In conclusion, a few key elements are really all you need

THE SUCCESS METHOD

6 Steps to Successful Crate Training

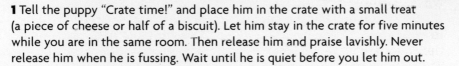

1 Tell the puppy "Crate time!" and place him in the crate with a small treat (a piece of cheese or half of a biscuit). Let him stay in the crate for five minutes while you are in the same room. Then release him and praise lavishly. Never release him when he is fussing. Wait until he is quiet before you let him out.

2 Repeat Step 1 several times a day.

3 The next day, place the puppy in the crate as before. Let him stay there for ten minutes. Do this several times.

4 Continue building time in five-minute increments until the puppy stays in his crate for 30 minutes with you in the room. Always take him to his relief area after prolonged periods in his crate.

5 Now go back to Step 1 and let the puppy stay in his crate for five minutes, this time while you are out of the room.

6 Once again, build crate time in five-minute increments with you out of the room. When the puppy will stay willingly in his crate (he may even fall asleep!) for 30 minutes with you out of the room, he will be ready to stay in it for several hours at a time.

PRACTICE MAKES PERFECT!

- Have training lessons with your dog every day in several short segments—three to five times a day for a few minutes at a time is ideal.
- Do not have long practice sessions. The dog will become easily bored.
- Never practice when you are tired, ill, worried or in an otherwise negative mood. This will transmit to the dog and may have an adverse effect on his performance.

　Think fun, short and above all *positive!* End each session on a high note, rather than a failed exercise, and make sure to give a lot of praise. Enjoy the training and help your dog enjoy it, too.

for a successful crate-training method—consistency, frequency, praise, control and supervision. By following these procedures with a normal, healthy puppy, you and the puppy will soon be past the stage of "accidents" and ready to move on to a full and rewarding life together.

ROLES OF DISCIPLINE, REWARD AND PUNISHMENT

Discipline, training one to act in accordance with rules, brings order to life. It is as simple as that. Without discipline, particularly in a group society, chaos reigns supreme and the group will eventually perish. Humans and canines are social animals and need some form of discipline in order to function effectively. They must procure food, reproduce to keep the species going and protect their home base and their young.

　If there were no discipline in the lives of social animals, they would eventually die from starvation and/or predation by other stronger animals. In the case of domestic canines, dogs need discipline in their lives in order to understand how their pack (you and other family members) function and how they must act in order to survive.

　A large humane society in a highly populated area recently surveyed dog owners regarding their satisfaction with their relationships with their dogs. People

who had trained their dogs were 75% more satisfied with their pets than those who had never trained their dogs.

Dr. Edward Thorndike, a noted psychologist, established *Thorndike's Theory of Learning*, which states that a behavior that results in a pleasant event tends to be repeated. Likewise, a behavior that results in an unpleasant event tends not to be repeated. It is this theory on which training methods are based today. For example, if you manipulate a dog to perform a specific behavior and reward him for doing it, he is likely to do it again because he enjoyed the end result.

Occasionally, punishment, a penalty inflicted for an offense, is necessary. The best type of punishment often comes from an outside source. For example, a child is told not to touch the stove because he may get burned. He

disobeys and touches the stove. In doing so, he receives a burn. From that time on, he respects the heat of the stove and avoids contact with it. Therefore, a behavior that results in an unpleasant event tends not to be repeated.

A good example of a dog learning the hard way is the dog who chases the house cat. He is told many times to leave the cat alone, yet he persists in teasing the cat. Then, one day he begins chasing the cat but the cat turns and swipes a claw across the dog's face, leaving him with a painful gash on his nose. The final result is that the dog stops chasing the cat.

TRAINING EQUIPMENT

COLLAR
A simple buckle collar is fine for most dogs. One who pulls mightily on the leash may require a

Reward your dog with praise and attention if he performs and behaves properly.

The selection of the collar for your Pit Bull depends upon the character of the dog and how well trained he is.

A favorite treat is sure to keep your Pit Bull motivated and focused on the lesson.

that switching the leash back and forth frequently between their hands is painful.

TREATS

Have a bag of treats on hand. Something nutritious and easy to swallow works best; use a soft treat, a chunk of cheese or a piece of cooked chicken rather than a dry biscuit. By the time the dog gets done chewing a dry treat, he will forget why he is being rewarded in the first place! Using food rewards will not teach a dog to beg at the table—the only way to teach a dog to beg at the table is to give him food from the table. In training, rewarding the dog with a food treat away from the table will help him associate praise and the treats with learning new behaviors that obviously please his owner.

chain choke collar. Only in the most severe cases of a dog's being totally out of control is it recommended to use a prong or pinch collar, and in this case only if the owner has been instructed in the proper use of such equipment. In some areas, these types of collars are not allowed.

LEASH

About a 6-foot leash is recommended, preferably made of leather, nylon or heavy cloth. A chain leash is not recommended, as many dog owners find that the chain cuts into their hands and

TRAINING BEGINS: ASK THE DOG A QUESTION

In order to teach your dog anything, you must first get his attention. After all, he cannot learn anything if he is looking away from you with his mind on something else.

To get his attention, ask him "School?" and immediately walk over to him and give him a treat as you tell him "Good dog." Wait a minute or two and repeat the routine, this time with a treat in your hand as you approach the dog to within a foot of him. Do not go directly to him, but stop

HOW TO WEAN THE "TREAT HOG"

If you have trained your dog by rewarding him with a treat each time he performs a command, he may soon decide that without the treat, he won't sit, stay or come. The best way to fix this problem is to start asking your dog to do certain commands twice before being rewarded. Slowly increase the number of commands given and then vary the number: three sits and a treat one day, five sits for a biscuit the next day, etc. Your dog will soon realize that there is no set number of sits before he gets his reward and he'll likely do it the first time you ask in the hope of being rewarded sooner rather than later.

him. In other words, he learns that "school" means doing fun things with you that result in treats and positive attention.

Remember that the dog does not understand your verbal language, he only recognizes sounds. Your question translates to a series of sounds for him, and those sounds become the signal to go to you and pay attention; if he does, he will get to interact with you plus receive treats and praise.

THE BASIC COMMANDS

TEACHING SIT

Now that you have the dog's attention, hold the leash in your left hand and the food treat in your right. Place your food hand at the dog's nose and let him lick

about a foot short of him and hold out the treat as you ask "School?" He will see you approaching with a treat in your hand and most likely begin walking toward you. As you meet, give him the treat and praise again.

The third time, ask the question, have a treat in your hand and walk only a short distance toward the dog so that he must walk almost all the way to you. As he reaches you, give him the treat and praise again.

By this time, the dog will be getting the idea that if he pays attention to you, especially when you ask that question, it will pay off in treats and fun activities for

Teaching your dog to sit is a fairly simple exercise; from there, you can progress to the sit/stay.

DOUBLE JEOPARDY

A dog in jeopardy never lies down. He stays alert on his feet because instinct tells him that he may have to run away or fight for his survival. Therefore, if a dog feels threatened or anxious, he will not lie down. Consequently, it is important to keep the dog calm and relaxed as he learns the down exercise.

the treat but not take it from you. Say "Sit" and slowly raise your food hand from in front of the dog's nose up over his head so that he is looking at the ceiling. As he bends his head upward, he will have to bend his knees to maintain his balance. As he bends his knees, he will assume a sit position. At that point, release the food treat and praise lavishly with comments such as "Good dog! Good sit!", etc. Remember to always praise enthusiastically, because dogs relish verbal praise from their owners and feel so proud of themselves whenever they accomplish a behavior.

You will not use food forever in getting the dog to obey your commands. Food is only used to teach new behaviors, and once the dog knows what you want when you give a specific command, you will wean him off of the food treats but still maintain the verbal praise. After all, you will always have your voice with you, but there will be many times when you have no food rewards yet you expect the dog to obey.

TEACHING DOWN

Teaching the down exercise is easy when you understand how the dog perceives the down position, and it is very difficult when you do not. In addition, teaching the down exercise using the wrong method can sometimes make the dog develop such a fear of the down that he either runs away when you say "Down" or he attempts to bite the person who tries to force him down.

Have the dog sit alongside your left leg, facing in the same direction as you are. Hold the leash in your left hand and a food treat in your right. Now place your left hand lightly on the top of the dog's shoulders where they meet above the spinal cord. Do not push down on the dog's shoulders; simply rest your left hand there so you can guide the dog to lie down close to your left leg rather than to swing away from your side when he drops.

LANGUAGE BARRIER

Dogs do not understand our language and have to rely on tone of voice more than just words or sound. They can be trained to react to a certain sound, at a certain volume. If you say "No, Oliver" in a very soft, pleasant voice, it will not have the same meaning as "No, Oliver!!" when you raise your voice. You should never use the dog's name during a reprimand, just the command "No! " You never want the dog to associate his name with a negative experience or reprimand.

Now place the food hand at the dog's nose, say "Down" very softly (almost a whisper) and slowly lower the food hand to the dog's front feet. When the food hand reaches the floor, begin moving it forward along the floor in front of the dog. Keep talking softly to the dog, saying things like, "Do you want this treat? You can do this, good dog." Your reassuring tone of voice will help calm the dog as he tries to follow the food hand to get the treat.

When the dog's elbows touch the floor, release the food and praise softly. Try to get the dog to maintain that down position for several seconds before you let him sit up again. The goal here is to get the dog to settle down and not feel threatened in the down position.

TEACHING STAY

It is easy to teach the dog to stay in either a sit or a down position. Again, we use food and praise during the teaching process as we help the dog to understand exactly what it is that we are expecting him to do.

To teach the sit/stay, start with the dog sitting on your left side as before and hold the leash in your left hand. Have a food treat in your right hand and place your food hand at the dog's nose. Say "Stay" and step out on your right foot to stand directly in front of the dog, toe to toe, as he licks and nibbles the treat. Be sure to keep his head facing upward to maintain the sit position. Count to five and then swing around to stand next to the dog again with him on your left. As soon as you get back to the original position, release the food and praise lavishly.

The stay exercise is taught using a combination of verbal commands and hand signals.

"WHERE ARE YOU?"

When calling the dog, do not say "Come." Say things like, "Rover, where are you? See if you can find me! I have a biscuit for you!" Keep up a constant line of chatter with coaxing sounds and frequent questions such as "Where are you?" The dog will learn to follow the sound of your voice to locate you and receive his reward.

To teach the down/stay, do the down as previously described. As soon as the dog lies down, say "Stay" and step out on your right foot just as you did in the sit/stay. Count to five and then return to stand beside the dog with him on your left side. Release the treat and praise as always.

Within a week or ten days, you can begin to add a bit of distance between you and your dog when you leave him. When you do, use your left hand open with the palm facing the dog as a stay signal, much the same as the hand signal a police officer uses

to stop traffic at an intersection. Hold the food treat in your right hand as before, but this time the food is not touching the dog's nose. He will watch the food hand and quickly learn that he is going to get that treat as soon as you return to his side.

When you can stand 3 feet away from your dog for 30 seconds, you can then begin building time and distance in both stays. Eventually, the dog can be expected to remain in the stay position for prolonged periods of time until you return to him or call him to you. Always praise lavishly when he stays.

TEACHING COME

If you make teaching "come" a fun experience, you should never have a student that does not love the game or that fails to come when called. The secret, it seems, is never to teach the word "come."

At times when an owner most wants his dog to come when called, the owner is likely upset or anxious and he allows these feelings to come through in the tone of his voice when he calls his dog. Hearing that desperation in his owner's voice, the dog fears the results of going to him and therefore either disobeys outright or runs in the opposite direction. The secret, therefore, is to teach the dog a game and, when you want him to come to you, simply play the game. It is practically a no-fail solution!

To begin, have several members of your family take a few food treats and each go into a different room in the house. Take turns calling the dog, and each person should celebrate the dog's finding him with a treat and lots of happy praise. When a person calls the dog, he is actually inviting the dog to find him and get a treat as a reward for "winning."

A few turns of the "Where are you?" game and the dog will figure out that everyone is playing the game and that each person has a big celebration awaiting the dog's success at locating them. Once he learns to love the game, simply calling out "Where are you?" will bring the dog running from wherever he is when he hears that all-important question.

The come command is recognized as one of the most important things to teach a dog, so it is interesting to note that there are trainers who work with thousands of dogs and never teach the actual

word "come." Yet these dogs will race to respond to a person who uses the dog's name followed by "Where are you?" For example, a woman has a 12-year-old companion dog who went blind, but who never fails to locate her owner when asked, "Where are you?"

Children particularly love to play this game with their dogs. Children can hide in smaller places like a shower stall or bathtub, behind a bed or under a table. The dog needs to work a little bit harder to find these hiding places, but, when he does, he loves to celebrate with a treat and a tussle with a favorite youngster.

TEACHING HEEL

Heeling means that the dog walks beside the owner without pulling. It takes time and patience on the owner's part to succeed at teaching the dog that he (the owner) will not

Teaching your dog to heel rewards you with a dog that you can control reliably on leash.

proceed unless the dog is walking calmly beside him. Pulling out ahead on the leash is definitely not acceptable.

Begin with holding the leash in your left hand as the dog sits beside your left leg. Hold the loop end of the leash in your right hand but keep your left hand short on the leash so it keeps the dog in close next to you.

Say "Heel" and step forward on your left foot. Keep the dog close to you and take three steps. Stop and have the dog sit next to you in what we now call the heel position. Praise verbally, but do not touch the dog. Hesitate a moment and begin again with "Heel," taking three steps and stopping, at which point the dog is told to sit again.

Your goal here is to have the dog walk those three steps with-

Reinforce polite behavior by having the dog sit every time you put his collar and leash on or take them off.

> **OBEDIENCE SCHOOL**
>
> Taking your dog to an obedience school may be the best investment in time and money you can ever make. You will enjoy the benefits for the lifetime of your dog and you will have the opportunity to meet people who have similar expectations for their companion dogs.

out pulling on the leash. When he will walk calmly beside you for three steps without pulling, increase the number of steps you take to five. When he will walk politely beside you while you take five steps, you can increase the length of your walk to ten steps. Keep increasing the length of your stroll until the dog will walk quietly beside you without pulling as long as you want him to heel. When you stop heeling, indicate to the dog that the exercise is over by verbally praising as you pet him and say "OK, good dog." The "OK" is used as a release word, meaning that the exercise is finished and the dog is free to relax.

If you are dealing with a dog who insists on pulling you around, simply "put on your brakes" and stand your ground until the dog realizes that the two of you are not going anywhere until he is beside you and moving at your pace, not his. It may take some time just standing there to

Always use praise along with food treats; that way, once you've weaned your dog from the treats, he will still look forward to being rewarded with your attention.

CONSISTENCY PAYS OFF

Dogs need consistency in their feeding schedule, exercise and relief visits, and in the verbal commands you use. If you use "Stay" on Monday and "Stay here, please" on Tuesday, you will confuse your dog. Don't demand perfect behavior during training sessions and then let him have the run of the house the rest of the day. Above all, lavish praise on your pet consistently every time he does something right. The more he feels he is pleasing you, the more willing he will be to learn.

convince the dog that you are the leader and you will be the one to decide on the direction and speed of your travel.

Each time the dog looks up at you or slows down to give a slack leash between the two of you, quietly praise him and say, "Good heel. Good dog." Eventually, the dog will begin to respond and within a few days he will be walking politely beside you without pulling on the leash. At first, the training sessions should be kept short and very positive; soon the dog will be able to walk nicely with you for increasingly longer distances. Remember also to give the dog free time and the opportunity to run and play when you are done with heel practice.

WEANING OFF FOOD IN TRAINING

Food is used in training new behaviors, yet once the dog understands what behavior goes with a specific command, it is time to start weaning him off the food treats. At first, give a treat after each exercise. Then, start to give a treat only after every other exercise. Mix up the times when you offer a food reward and the times when you only offer praise so that the dog will never know when he is going to receive both food and praise and when he is going to receive only praise. This is called a variable ratio reward system and it proves successful because there is always the chance that the owner will produce a treat, so the dog never stops trying for that reward. No matter what, *always* give verbal praise.

Give your Pit Bull pup love, guidance and positive reinforcement from the very beginning to mold him into a loyal and dependable companion.

A BORN PRODIGY

Occasionally, a dog and owner who have not attended formal classes have been able to earn entry-level obedience titles by obtaining competition rules and regulations from a local kennel club and practicing on their own to a degree of perfection. Obtaining the higher level titles, however, almost always requires extensive training under the tutelage of experienced instructors. In addition, the more difficult levels require more specialized equipment whereas the lower levels do not.

OBEDIENCE CLASSES

As previously discussed, it is a good idea to enroll in an obedience class if one is available in your area. Many areas have dog clubs that offer basic obedience training as well as preparatory classes for obedience competition. There are also local dog trainers who offer similar classes.

At obedience trials, dogs can earn titles at various levels of competition. The beginning levels of competition include basic behaviors such as sit, down, heel, etc. The more advanced levels of competition include jumping, retrieving, scent discrimination and signal work. The advanced levels require a dog and owner to put a lot of time and effort into their training; the titles that can be earned at these levels of competition are very prestigious.

Activities for You and Your American Pit Bull Terrier

Whether a dog is trained in the structured environment of a class or alone with his owner at home, there are many activities that can bring fun and rewards to both owner and dog once they have mastered basic control.

Teaching the dog to help out around the home, in the garden or on the farm provides great satisfaction to both dog and owner. In addition, the dog's help makes life a little easier for his owner and raises his stature as a valued companion to his family. It helps give the dog a purpose; it helps to keep his mind occupied and provides an outlet for his energy.

If you are interested in participating in organized competition with your Pit Bull, there are other activities other than obedience in

which you and your dog can become involved. Agility is a popular and fun sport in which dogs run through an obstacle course that includes various jumps, tunnels and other exercises to test the dog's speed and coordination. The owners often run through the course beside their dogs to give commands and to guide them through the course. Although competitive, the focus is on fun—it's fun to do and fun to watch, as well as great exercise.

Children and dogs make natural friends. One of the best ways to develop the bond is by participating in activities that both the child and the dog can enjoy.

BACKPACKING

Backpacking is an exciting and healthful activity that the dog can be taught without assistance from more than his owner. The exercise of walking and climbing is good for man and dog alike, and the bond that they develop together is priceless. Don't allow the dog to carry more than one-sixth of his body weight.

WALKING

The first form of exercise that the average Pit Bull owner should consider is simply walking the dog on a very regular basis. What constitutes a walk? Well, the ideal

The Pit Bull is a
fine companion
dog who will
welcome partici-
pating in activi-
ties and spending
time with all
members of the
family.

The Pit Bull is a fine companion dog who will welcome participating in activities and spending time with all members of the family.

dog-walking scenario is one in which both owner and dog take a brisk walk on a hard surface. The ideal surface is simple concrete such as that of the average sidewalk. Concrete is good for the dog because in addition to taking a healthy walk, the dog is also being groomed. As the dog walks, his nails are being worn down as if they were being filed. In fact, a good rule of thumb is that if you ever need to file or clip your dog's nails, you know the dog is not being walked enough.

A good healthy walk for an adult Pit Bull would be a brisk three-mile walk. A longer walk would be even better for both the dog and the walker. Such walks should occur at least four times a week and, if possible, daily (weather permitting). The best time of the day for such a walk is early evening, after the sun has gone down. Walks on very hot days should either be avoided or the person walking with the dog should be ever aware of the effect of the heat on the dog. If the weather is warm and the dog begins to appear uncomfortable, the walk should be called off. If the weather is cold and dry, a brisk walk should be fine for the dog. While the Pit Bull is not the kind of dog that you should

STAYING IN SHAPE
Through the generations, the activity for which Pit Bulls were produced demanded that these dogs be kept very physically fit. Just as any human fighter needs months of intense training before facing an opponent in the ring, the fighting Pit Bull also needed plenty of conditioning before being matched against an opponent. While the fighting aspect of Pit Bull history is not to be encouraged today, keeping the pet Pit Bull physically fit certainly is. Consider a few innovative ways to keep your Pit Bull in top physical condition.

Your Pit Bull must be exercised and should behave well on his leash no matter who takes him for walks.

WALKING FOR HEALTH
Dogs need to walk for fitness purposes. Unfortunately, sometimes dogs are owned by people who refuse to walk for any distance, in spite of the health benefits of walking for both dog and man. In such instances, the use of the dog treadmill is commonly employed when exercising Pit Bulls. Of course, the treadmill requires professional supervision and should not be utilized by novices.

maintain outdoors all year in colder climates, short-term exposure to the cold, especially during a brisk walk, will not adversely affect the dog. Also, if you feel comfortably cool during a long walk with your dog but the dog begins to look uncomfortably warm, stop walking and allow the dog to rest. Bear firmly in mind that the dog's natural pace is much faster than a human's, and such abnormally slow walks can lead to a dog's exhaustion more quickly than you might expect. Remember, the Pit Bull is not a breed that should be allowed to roam free! During all walks with the dog, the dog should be leashed.

When we see a Pit Bull harnessed to a treadmill, the underground activity of dog fighting generally leaps to mind. It is true that dog fighters often employ the treadmill to keep their fighting dogs fit, but it is also true that many Pit Bulls love to use treadmills for exercise purposes, just as a pet hamster enjoys running in its exercise wheel for no apparent reason. Dog treadmills come in two forms. The first is the lesser seen circular treadmill. Such treadmills are not generally practical for the average pet dog owner because they take up a great deal of space. In order to envision this type of treadmill, imagine a large record-player-type circular plate on rollers with a pole jutting through the center of the plate. The dog is leashed to the pole and it runs on the wheel for pure enjoyment. It will amaze you just how much a dog will enjoy this activity, in fact.

The second type is the rectangular treadmill. These mills are much like the treadmills that are commonly used by people. The dog is leashed to the top of the mill. The mill is often slanted slightly upward. The dog runs for pleasure. If the mill is inclined, the leash should be sufficiently long for the dog to get off the mill should he desire to do so. Again, just as we are often surprised at how much time our pet hamster will spend running in its exercise wheel, you may be surprised at how enjoyable your Pit Bull will find using his treadmill. Such treadmills can often be found in dog-supply shops that cater to Pit Bull owners.

BICYCLE RIDING
WITH YOUR PIT BULL

Bicycle riding with your Pit Bull is an activity I suggest with great reservation. While a dog's natural pace is closer to a person's casual bike-riding speed than it is to a person's natural walking pace, the dog must always remain leashed. It's fairly easy to take an embarrassing spill while trying to ride a bicycle while leashed to a dog, and such spills can be more than just embarrassing, they can be dangerous. And don't underestimate the strength of a Pit Bull—if you're concentrating on riding and the dog suddenly decides that he doesn't want to go in that direction or that he doesn't want to go anywhere at all, you're going to have a problem. Bike riding with a dog must be undertaken with the utmost caution, so it's not an activity that comes highly recommended.

PLAYTIME WITH OTHER DOGS

Another good form of occasional exercise for the Pit Bull is a little friendly play with another dog. It cannot be emphasized enough that the other dog chosen to participate in playtime with your Pit Bull must be one that is well known to your dog, one that is not too small, one that is always friendly to your dog and one to which your dog is always friendly. Even under these conditions, play between the Pit Bull

and another dog should always be carefully supervised and the owners of both dogs should always be present. Play between the Pit Bull and more than one other dog at a time is discouraged.

WEIGHT PULLING

A form of exercise that can be recommended for the Pit Bull is really something that only a small segment of the Pit-Bull-owning

PLAYMATES

It seems that the most strenuous play between two dogs is that of two dogs who know each other well but do not live together. Dogs living together tend to take each other for granted. Dogs that see each other only occasionally tend to seize the opportunity to play hard when they can. While organizing this type of structured play may not be convenient every day, the occasional hard play session is good for exercising your dog as well as for socializing your dog. Let the dogs enjoy themselves when possible.

population will be interested in, but perhaps the reader is part of that small segment. This form of exercise is weight pulling. Just as many people lift weights to keep themselves not just in good condition, but in *peak* condition, many Pit Bull owners like to keep their dogs in peak condition. Such owners may be interested in involving their dogs in regular weight-pulling exercises.

Before discussing weight-pulling exercises for your dog, you should understand a few things. The first is that the Pit Bull breed is not and has never been a weight-pulling dog. This is to say that weight pulling was never an activity for which this breed was selectively bred. Other breeds were and continue to be selectively bred for their ability to pull weights, the sled dogs being the best example of such breeds.

Nonetheless, there is nothing fundamentally wrong with involving your Pit Bull in weight pulls for fun, sport and exercise. The reader should be aware that

A Pit Bull in fit condition is all muscle. He loves to run, jump and play. Pit Bulls are fun and versatile companions.

due to the association of the Pit Bull breed with the activity of dog fighting, other dog fanciers may misinterpret or resent your interest in this activity. This can lead to an awkward situation such as the one that occurred in the following anecdote.

To make a long story short, there was a man who owned a very large, blocky and powerful Pit Bull. A weightlifter himself, he began to involve his dog in weight pulling. The dog loved it so much that, one evening, the man decided to show a friend just how much the dog enjoyed pulling. In order to do this, he harnessed the dog to a small car, let up the car's emergency brake, stood about 20 feet in front of the dog and began to yell words of encouragement to the dog, who had never pulled a car and was, at first, not sure what to do. Shortly after the man began yelling to the dog and the dog began to pull, a woman began screaming out of the window of a nearby apartment building that she was going to call the police to report cruelty to the dog! Within minutes, the police arrived, and they watched in amazement as the dog pulled the car. After watching for a while, one of the police officers declared that he was going to buy himself a Pit Bull and they drove away. Still, it is best to avoid making the negative

The naturally muscular Pit Bull is well-suited to exercises requiring strength and stamina.

impression that was undoubtedly made upon this woman, for the sake of the breed.

Should you decide to begin training your Pit Bull for weight pulling, you will need a few things. First, you will probably want an indoor location, so as to avoid the kind of conflict just described. Second, you will need some carpeting so the dog won't hurt his paws while pulling. A carpet that is not very plush is best for this; indoor/outdoor carpeting is ideal. Third, you will need a cart with wheels and a low flat top. Such a cart can be built easily enough. It should not be very wide and the wheels should be 6 inches in diameter or so. Larger wheels will make for an easier pull. If you want to get serious about weight-pulling competitions, find whatever local club sponsors weight-pulling events for dogs and be sure to construct a cart that meets the club's standards for competition.

Fourth, you will need weights. Bricks or cinder blocks are fine, but the kind of weightlifting plates that people use are best.

If the dog owner is a weightlifter himself, this will not require the purchase of additional weights; if not, the weights can be obtained easily enough from a sporting-goods store.

Finally, you will need a harness to attach the cart to the dog. Such harnesses are often available through magazines that cater to Pit Bull owners, but a comfortable leather harness can also be made by a leather worker who deals with horses. If you intend to have a harness made just for weight pulling, start the dog off with wearing the harness before you introduce the animal to actually pulling weights. Allow the dog time to associate the harness with positive events like a

It's helpful to have a friend involved, one whom the dog knows well, when introducing your Pit Bull to new activities.

short walk. Once the dog is comfortable with the harness, or with one like it, you can begin to use the harness for cart pulling.

It's best to have two people present during weight-pulling exercises. Begin by harnessing the dog to the cart with no weights on the cart. Have a friend (one who knows the dog and with whom the dog is familiar) hold the harnessed dog on the carpet while you, the dog's owner, take a position a few yards in front of the dog. Simultaneously release the dog and begin to encourage him to come to you. If the dog looks confused and does not move, encourage him more. If the dog refuses to come, end the session and try again another day. You might also try sitting in your position, acting casual and waiting for the dog to come to you. Often a little gentle encouragement is easier to comprehend than an overwhelming onslaught of encouragement.

When the dog finally pulls the empty cart in order to come to you, act excited and praise the dog profusely. Try the pull again and again. Use no weights on the first day of pulling unless the dog is very obviously enjoying himself, which some dogs do. As the dog becomes familiar with the routine, begin to add weight to the cart. Start off with light weights and, when the dog has learned to pull these with enthusiasm, begin an actual training routine.

A training routine can be easily devised. An example of such a routine follows; you can adapt it according to your personal schedule and situation.

Work out a weekly schedule and stick to it. On one day, load the cart with as much weight as the dog can pull 8 or even 10 times over a distance of roughly 5 yards. Encourage the dog to pull the weight for the amount of repetitions you have decided on (we'll use 8 as an example). The dog should be allowed to rest for about a minute between each repetition. When this has been accomplished, allow the dog to rest for three minutes, increase the weight to whatever the dog can pull for six repetitions and follow the procedure above.

When this has been accomplished, increase the weight again to whatever the dog can pull for four repetitions. When this has been accomplished, allow the dog to rest for three minutes. Finally, encourage the dog to pull as much weight as he can pull twice. This should be the heaviest weight pulled that day.

On the second day, rest the dog. On the third day, follow the routine for the first day. On the fourth and fifth days, allow the dog to rest. On the sixth day, begin the dog with the weight he can pull for six repetitions and follow the schedule as you have

This Pit Bull looks like he is ready for action! Try out some different activities until you find which ones your dog likes best.

been. When the dog has made his final two pulls, increase the weight and encourage the dog to pull a maximum weight one time only. If the dog can pull that maximum weight twice, all weights should be increased. On the seventh day, rest. Each day you should give the dog a brisk one-mile walk before and after the pulling session.

That should get you and your dog started. Remember, just as with any strenuous exercise you may do yourself, after the first day or two of a new exercise, muscles will be sore. Allow for some extra rest time in the beginning. Also, should you find that your dog simply doesn't enjoy weight pulling, forget it and concentrate on one of the other forms of exercise that he does enjoy. Again, it should be reiterated that weight pulling is not what this breed was originally intended for and, as such, your Pit Bull may just not take to it.

Your Pit Bull's crate is where he belongs under unfamiliar circumstances, like a visit to the vet. Crates should be sturdy and easy to transport.

Health Care of Your American Pit Bull Terrier

Dogs suffer from many of the same physical illnesses as people and might even share many of the same psychological problems. Since people usually know more about human diseases than canine maladies, many of the terms used in this chapter will be familiar but not necessarily those used by veterinarians. For example, we will use the familiar term *x-ray* instead of *radiograph*. We will also use the familiar term *symptoms*, even though dogs don't have symptoms, which are verbal descriptions of something the patient feels or observes himself that he regards as abnormal. Dogs have *clinical signs* since they cannot speak, so we have to look for these clinical signs...but we still use the term *symptoms* in the book.

Medicine is a constantly changing art, with some scientific input as well. Things alter as we learn more and more about basic sciences such as genetics and biochemistry, and have use of more sophisticated imaging techniques like Computer Aided Tomography (CAT scans) or Magnetic Resonance Imaging (MRI scans). There is academic

Broken bones, dysplasia and other bone problems are diagnosed by x-rays. Your vet should be trained in the taking and reading of x-rays.

dispute about many canine maladies, so different vets treat them in different ways, and some vets place a greater emphasis on surgical treatment than others.

SELECTING A QUALIFIED VET

Your selection of a veterinarian should be based on personal recommendation for his skills with animals, especially dogs, and, if possible, especially Pit Bulls or similar breeds. If the vet is based nearby, it will be helpful because you might have an emergency or need to make multiple visits for treatments.

All veterinarians are licensed and should be capable of dealing with routine medical issues such as infections, injuries and the promotion of health (for example,

Your Pit Bull's teeth must be checked regularly as part of his check-ups, and you should initiate a dental-care routine at home.

by vaccination). If the problem affecting your dog is more complex, your vet will refer your pet to someone with a more detailed knowledge of what is wrong. This will usually be a specialist who concentrates in a specific field, such as heart problems (veterinary cardiologist), skin problems (veterinary dermatologist), tooth and gum problems (veterinary dentist), eye problems (veterinary ophthalmologist), cancers (veterinary oncologist), etc, whatever is relevant to your dog's problem. There are also surgeons who have specialties in skin, bones or certain organs.

Veterinary procedures are very costly and as the treatments available improve, they are going to become more expensive. It is quite acceptable to discuss matters of cost with your vet; if there is more than one treatment option, cost may be a factor in deciding which route to take.

Insurance against veterinary cost is also becoming very popular. This will not pay for routine vaccinations, but will cover the costs for unexpected emergencies such as emergency surgery after a car accident.

PREVENTATIVE MEDICINE

It is much easier, less costly and more effective to practice preventative medicine than to fight bouts of illness and disease. Properly bred puppies of all breeds come from parents that were selected based upon their genetic-disease profiles. The puppies' mother should have been vaccinated, free of all internal and external parasites and properly nourished. For these reasons, a visit to the veterinarian who cared for the dam is recommended, if possible. The dam passes on disease resistance to her puppies, which should last from eight to ten weeks. Unfortunately, she can also pass on parasites and infection. This is why knowledge about her health is useful in learning more about the health of the puppies.

WEANING TO FIVE MONTHS OLD

Puppies should be weaned by the time they are two months old. A puppy that remains for at least eight weeks with his mother and littermates usually adapts better to other dogs and people later in his life.

Sometimes new owners have their puppy examined by a vet immediately, which is a good idea unless the puppy is overtired by a

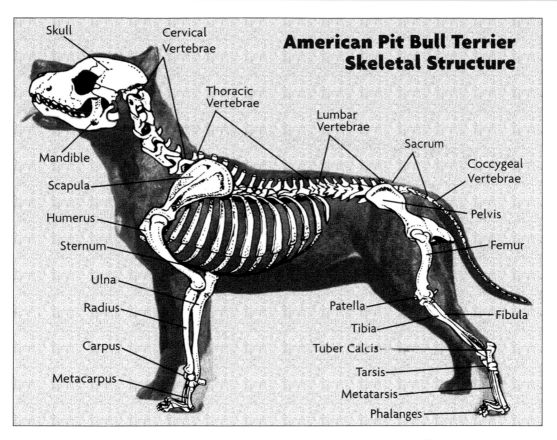

American Pit Bull Terrier Skeletal Structure

Skull

Cervical Vertebrae

Thoracic Vertebrae

Lumbar Vertebrae

Sacrum

Coccygeal Vertebrae

Mandible

Scapula

Humerus

Sternum

Ulna

Radius

Carpus

Metacarpus

Pelvis

Femur

Patella

Fibula

Tibia

Tuber Calcis

Tarsis

Metatarsis

Phalanges

long journey. In that case, plan to take the pup to the vet in the next day or two after bringing him home.

The puppy will have his teeth examined and have his skeletal conformation and general health checked prior to certification by the veterinarian. Puppies in certain breeds have problems with their kneecaps, cataracts and other eye problems, heart murmurs and undescended testicles. Your vet also might have training in temperament testing and evaluation. During the first visit, the vet will also set up a schedule for continuing the pup's vaccinations.

VACCINATIONS

Most vaccinations are given by injection and should only be given by a veterinarian. Both he and you should keep a record of the date of the injection, the identification of the vaccine and the amount given. Some vets give a first vaccination at eight weeks, but most dog breeders prefer the

HEALTH AND VACCINATION SCHEDULE

Age in Weeks:	3rd	6th	8th	10th	12th	14th	16th	20-24th
Worm Control	✔	✔	✔	✔	✔	✔	✔	✔
Neutering								✔
Heartworm		✔						✔
Parvovirus		✔		✔		✔		✔
Distemper			✔		✔		✔	
Hepatitis			✔		✔		✔	
Leptospirosis		✔		✔		✔		
Parainfluenza		✔		✔		✔		
Dental Examination			✔					✔
Complete Physical			✔					✔
Temperament Testing			✔					
Coronavirus					✔			
Kennel Cough		✔						
Hip Dysplasia							✔	
Rabies								✔

Vaccinations are not instantly effective. It takes about two weeks for the dog's immune system to develop antibodies. Most vaccinations require annual booster shots. Your vet should guide you in this regard.

course not to commence until about ten weeks because of the risk of interaction with the antibodies produced by the mother. The vaccination timetable is usually based on a 15-day cycle. You must take your vet's advice as to when to vaccinate, as this may differ according to the vaccine used and according to the vaccinations the pup received while still with the breeder.

The usual vaccines contain immunizing doses of several different viruses such as distemper, parvovirus, parainfluenza and hepatitis. There are other vaccines available when the puppy is at risk. You should rely upon professional advice. This is especially true for the booster immunizations. Most vaccination programs require a booster when the puppy is a year old and once a year thereafter. In some cases, circumstances may require more or less frequent immunizations.

Kennel cough, more formally known as tracheobronchitis, is immunized against with a vaccine that is sprayed into the dog's nostrils. Kennel cough is usually included in routine vaccination, but it is often not as effective as the vaccines for other major diseases.

FIVE MONTHS TO ONE YEAR OF AGE
Unless you intend to breed or
show your dog, neutering the
puppy around six months of age
is recommended. Discuss this
with your veterinarian. Neutering/
spaying has proven to be
extremely beneficial to male and
female dogs, respectively. Besides
eliminating the possibility of
pregnancy, it inhibits (but does
not prevent) breast cancer in
bitches and prostate cancer in
male dogs. Opinions about the
best age at which to neuter or
spay may differ between breeders
and vets, so this is something
you should discuss.

Your veterinarian should
provide your puppy with a thorough dental evaluation at six
months of age, ascertaining
whether all of the permanent
teeth have erupted properly. A
home dental-care regimen should
be initiated at six months,
including brushing weekly and
providing good dental chew
devices (such as hard plastic or
nylon bones). Regular dental care
promotes healthy teeth, fresh
breath and a longer life.

DOGS OLDER THAN ONE YEAR
Continue to visit the veterinarian
at least once a year. There is no
such disease as "old age," but
bodily functions do change with
age. The eyes and ears are no
longer as efficient. Liver, kidney
and intestinal functions often

decline. Proper dietary changes,
recommended by your vet, can
make life more pleasant for your
aging Pit Bull and you.

SKIN PROBLEMS
Vets are consulted by dog owners
for skin problems more than for
any other group of diseases or
maladies. A dog's skin is as
sensitive, if not more so, than
human skin, and both suffer
from almost the same ailments
(though the occurrence of acne
in most breeds is rare!). For this
reason, veterinary dermatology
has developed into a specialty
practiced by many vets.

Since many skin problems
have visual symptoms that are
almost identical, it requires the
skill of an experienced veterinary dermatologist to identify
and cure many of the more
severe skin disorders. Pet shops
sell many treatments for skin
problems, but most of the treatments are directed at symptoms
and not at the underlying prob-
lem(s). If your dog is suffering
from a skin disorder, you should
seek professional assistance as
quickly as possible. As with all
diseases, the earlier a problem is
identified and treated, the more
likely it is that the cure will be
successful.

HEREDITARY SKIN DISORDERS
Veterinary dermatologists are
currently researching a number

HOW TO PREVENT BLOAT

Research has confirmed that the structure of deep-chested breeds contributes to their predisposition to potentially deadly bloat. Nevertheless, there are several precautions that you can take to reduce the risk of this condition:

- Feed your dog twice daily rather than offer one big meal.
- Do not exercise your dog for at least one hour before and two hours after he has eaten.
- Make certain that your dog is calm and not overly excited while he is eating. It has been proven that nervous or overly excited dogs are more prone to develop bloat.
- Add a small portion of moist meat product to his dry food ration.
- Serve his meals in an elevated bowl stand, which avoids the dog's craning his neck while eating.
- To prevent your dog from gobbling his food too quickly, and thereby swallowing air, put some large (unswallowable) toys into his bowl so that he will have to eat around them to get his food.
- Never allow your dog to gulp water.

---

of skin disorders that are believed to have a hereditary basis. These inherited diseases are transmitted by both parents, who appear (phenotypically) normal but have a recessive gene for the disease, meaning that they carry, but are not affected by, the disease. These diseases pose serious problems to breeders because in some instances there are no methods of identifying carriers. Often the secondary diseases associated with these skin conditions are even more debilitating than the skin disorders themselves, including cancers and respiratory problems.

Among the hereditary skin disorders for which the mode of inheritance is known are acrodermatitis, cutaneous asthenia (Ehlers-Danlos syndrome), sebaceous adenitis, cyclic hematopoiesis, dermatomyositis, IgA deficiency, color dilution alopecia and nodular dermatofibrosis. Some of these disorders are limited to one or two breeds, while others affect a large number of breeds. All inherited diseases must be diagnosed and treated by a veterinary specialist.

PARASITE BITES

Many of us are allergic to insect bites. The bites itch, erupt and may even become infected. Dogs have the same reaction to fleas, ticks and/or mites. When an insect lands on you, you have the chance to whisk it away with your hand. Unfortunately, when a dog is bitten by a flea, tick or mite, he can only scratch it away or bite it. By the time the dog has been bitten, the parasite has done some of its damage. It may also have laid eggs, which will cause further problems in the near future. The itching from parasite bites is probably due to the saliva injected into the site when the parasite sucks the dog's blood.

AIRBORNE ALLERGIES

Just as humans suffer from hay fever during the pollinating season, many dogs suffer from the same allergies. When the pollen count is high, your dog might suffer, but don't expect him to sneeze and have a runny nose as a human would. Dogs react to pollen allergies in the same way they react to fleas—they scratch and bite themselves. Dogs, like humans, can be tested for allergens. Discuss the testing with your veterinarian.

ACRAL LICK GRANULOMA

The Pit Bull, as well as many breeds of similar size and larger,

DETECTING BLOAT

Bloat is a life-threatening condition in which the stomach twists around on itself. It is of utmost importance to recognize the symptoms, as it occurs suddenly and the dog's condition will worsen quickly. It is necessary for your Pit Bull to get immediate veterinary attention if you notice any of the following:

- Your dog's stomach starts to distend, ending up large and as tight as a football;
- Your dog is dribbling, as no saliva can be swallowed;
- Your dog makes frequent attempts to vomit but cannot bring anything up due to the stomach's being closed off;
- Your dog is distressed from pain;
- Your dog starts to suffer from clinical shock, meaning that there is not enough blood in the dog's circulation as the hard, dilated stomach stops the blood from returning to the heart to be pumped around the body. Clinical shock is indicated by pale gums and tongue, as they have been starved of blood. The shocked dog also has glazed, staring eyes.

You have minutes—yes, *minutes*—to get your dog into surgery. If you see any of these symptoms at any time of the day or night, get to the vet immediately. Someone will have to phone and warn that you are on your way (which is a justification for the invention of the cellular phone!) so that they can be prepared to get your pet on the operating table.

Check your Pit Bull's skin and coat regularly, as he runs the risk of encountering parasites, allergens and other irritants outdoors.

SIMULATED MEDICAL CONDITION FOR EDUCATIONAL PURPOSES ONLY.

Acral lick granuloma is evidenced by a raw, open wound, usually on the dog's front leg. can have a very poorly understood syndrome called acral lick granuloma. The manifestation of the problem is the dog's tireless attack at a specific area of the body, almost always the legs or paws. The dog licks so intensively that he removes the hair and skin, leaving an ugly, large wound. Tiny protuberances, which are outgrowths of new capillaries, bead on the surface of the wound. Owners who notice their dogs' biting and chewing at their extremities should have the vet determine the cause. If lick granuloma is identified, although there is no absolute cure, corticosteroids are the most common treatment.

AUTO-IMMUNE ILLNESSES

An auto-immune illness is one in which the immune system overacts and does not recognize parts of the affected person; rather, the immune system starts to react as if these parts were foreign and need to be destroyed. An example is rheumatoid arthritis, which occurs when the body does not recognize the joints, thus leading to a very painful and damaging reaction in the joints. This has nothing to do with age, so can occur in children. The wear-and-tear arthritis of the older person or dog is osteoarthritis.

Lupus is an auto-immune disease that affects dogs as well as people. It can take variable forms, affecting the kidneys, bones and the skin. It can be fatal, so is treated with steroids, which can themselves have very significant side effects. The steroids calm down the allergic reaction to the body's tissues, which helps the lupus, but also decrease the body's reaction to real foreign substances such as bacteria; steroids also thin the skin and bones.

FOOD PROBLEMS

FOOD ALLERGIES

Some dogs can be allergic to many foods that are best-sellers and highly recommended by breeders and veterinarians. Changing the brand of food that you buy may not eliminate the problem if the element to which the dog is allergic is contained in the new brand.

Recognizing a food allergy in a dog can be difficult. Humans often have rashes when they eat foods to which they are allergic, or have swelling of the lips or eyes. Dogs do not usually develop rashes, but react in the same way as they to an airborne or insect-bite allergy—they itch, scratch and bite themselves. While pollen allergies are usually seasonal, food allergies are year-round problems.

Diagnosis of food allergy is based on a two- to four-week dietary trial with a home-cooked diet fed to the exclusion of all other foods. The diet should consist of boiled rice or potato with a source of protein that the dog has never eaten before, such as fresh or frozen fish, lamb or even something as exotic as pheasant. Water has to be the only drink, and it is really important that no other foods are fed during this trial. If the dog's condition improves, you will need to try the original diet once again to see if the itching resumes. If it does, then this confirms the diagnosis that the dog is allergic to his original diet. The treatment is long-term feeding of something that does not distress the dog's skin, which may be in the form of one of the commercially avail-able hypoallergenic diets or the home-made diet that you created for the allergy trial.

FOOD INTOLERANCE

Food intolerance is the inability of the dog to completely digest certain foods. This occurs because the dog does not have the chemicals necessary to digest some foodstuffs. These chemicals are called enzymes. All puppies have the enzymes necessary to digest canine milk, but some dogs do not have the enzymes to digest a very different form of milk that is commonly found in human households—milk from cows. In such dogs, drinking cows' milk results in loose bowels, stomach pains and the passage of gas.

Dogs often do not have the enzymes to digest soy or other beans. The treatment is to exclude the foodstuffs that upset your Pit Bull's digestion.

A HEALTHY BREED

Fortunately, breeders report very few hereditary health problems in the American Pit Bull Terrier. Probably the biggest health concerns in the breed are those that are directly related to the Pit Bull's natural strength and high activity level. Some examples include injuries to muscles and joints, broken bones, torn ligaments and broken teeth.

A male dog flea, *Ctenocephalides canis.*

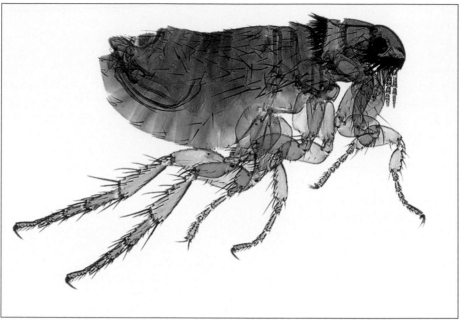

EXTERNAL PARASITES

FLEAS

Of all the problems to which dogs are prone, none is more well known and frustrating than fleas. Flea infestation is relatively simple to cure but difficult to prevent. Parasites that are harbored inside the body are a bit more difficult to eradicate but they are easier to control.

To control flea infestation, you have to understand the flea's life cycle. Fleas are often thought of as a summertime problem, but centrally heated homes have changed the patterns and fleas can be found at any time of the year. The most effective method of flea control is a two-stage approach: one stage to kill the adult fleas, and the other to control the development of pre-adult fleas. Unfortunately, no single active ingredient is effective against all stages of the life cycle.

FLEA KILLER CAUTION— "POISON"

Flea-killers are poisonous. You should not spray these toxic chemicals on areas of a dog's body that he licks, including his genitals and his face. Flea killers taken internally are a better answer, but check with your vet in case internal therapy is not advised for your dog.

LIFE CYCLE STAGES

During its life, a flea will pass through four life stages: egg, larva, pupa or nymph and adult. The adult stage is the most visible and irritating stage of the flea life cycle, and this is why the majority of flea-control products concentrate on this stage. The fact is that adult fleas account for only 1% of the total flea population, and the other 99% exist in pre-adult stages, i.e., eggs, larvae and nymphs. The pre-adult stages are barely visible to the naked eye.

THE LIFE CYCLE OF THE FLEA

Eggs are laid on the dog, usually in quantities of about 20 or 30, several times a day. The adult female flea must have a blood meal before each egg-laying session. When first laid, the eggs will cling to the dog's hair, as the eggs are still moist. However, they will quickly dry out and fall from the dog, especially if the dog moves around or scratches. Many eggs will fall off in the dog's favorite area or an area in which he spends a lot of time, such as his bed.

Once the eggs fall from the dog onto the carpet or furniture, they will hatch into larvae. This takes from one to ten days. Larvae are not particularly mobile and will usually travel only a few inches from where they hatch. However, they do have a tendency to move away from bright light and heavy

EN GARDE:
CATCHING FLEAS OFF GUARD!
Consider the following ways to arm yourself against fleas:

- Add a small amount of pennyroyal or eucalyptus oil to your dog's bath. These natural remedies repel fleas.
- Supplement your dog's food with fresh garlic (minced or grated) and an hearty amount of brewer's yeast, both of which ward off fleas.
- Use a flea comb on your dog daily. Submerge fleas in a cup of bleach to kill them quickly.
- Confine the dog to only a few rooms to limit the spread of fleas in the home.
- Vacuum daily...and get all of the crevices! Dispose of the bag every few days until the problem is under control.
- Wash your dog's bedding daily. Cover cushions where your dog sleeps with towels, and wash the towels often.

traffic—under furniture and behind doors are common places to find high quantities of flea larvae.

The flea larvae feed on dead organic matter, including adult flea feces, until they are ready to change into adult fleas. Fleas will usually remain as larvae for around seven days. After this period, the larvae will pupate into protective pupae. While inside the pupae, the larvae will undergo

Fleas have been measured as being able to jump 300,000 times and can jump 150 times their length in any direction, including straight up.

metamorphosis and change into adult fleas. This can take as little time as a few days, but the adult fleas can remain inside the pupae waiting to hatch for up to two years. The pupae are signaled to hatch by certain stimuli, such as physical pressure—the pupae's being stepped on, heat from an animal's lying on the pupae or increased carbon-dioxide levels and vibrations—indicating that a suitable host is available.

Once hatched, the adult flea must feed within a few days. Once the adult flea finds a host, it will not leave voluntarily. It only becomes dislodged by grooming or the host animal's scratching.

The adult flea will remain on the host for the duration of its life unless forcibly removed.

TREATING THE ENVIRONMENT AND THE DOG

Treating fleas should be a two-pronged attack. First, the environment needs to be treated; this includes carpets and furniture, especially the dog's bedding and areas underneath furniture. The environment should be treated with a household spray containing an Insect Growth Regulator (IGR) and an insecticide to kill the adult fleas. Most IGRs are effective against eggs and larvae; they actually mimic the fleas' own hormones and stop the eggs and larvae from developing into adult fleas. There are currently no treatments available to attack the pupa stage of the life cycle, so the adult insecticide is used to kill the newly hatched adult fleas before they find a host. Most IGRs are active for many months, while

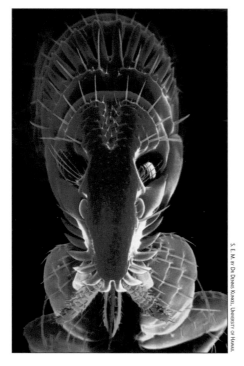

A scanning electron micrograph of a dog or cat flea, *Ctenocephalides,* magnified more than 100x. This image has been colorized for effect.

THE LIFE CYCLE OF THE FLEA

Adult

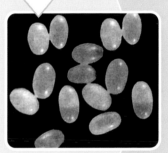

Egg

**Pupa
or
Nymph**

Larva

A LOOK AT FLEAS

Fleas have been around for millions of years and have adapted to changing host animals. They are able to go through a complete life cycle in less than one month or they can extend their lives to almost two years by remaining as pupae or cocoons. They do not need blood or any other food for up to 20 months.

INSECT GROWTH REGULATOR (IGR)

Two types of products should be used when treating fleas—a product to treat the pet and a product to treat the home. Adult fleas represent less than 1% of the flea population. The pre-adult fleas (eggs, larvae and pupae) represent more than 99% of the flea population and are found in the environment; it is in the case of pre-adult fleas that products containing an Insect Growth Regulator (IGR) should be used in the home.

IGRs are a new class of compounds used to prevent the development of insects. They do not kill the insect outright, but instead use the insect's biology against it to stop it from completing its growth. Products that contain methoprene are the world's first and leading IGRs. Used to control fleas and other insects, this type of IGR will stop flea larvae from developing and protect the house for up to seven months.

The American dog tick, *Dermacentor variabilis*, is probably the most common tick found on dogs. Look at the strength in its eight legs! No wonder it's hard to detach them.

The second stage of treatment is to apply an adult insecticide to the dog. Traditionally, this would be in the form of a collar or a spray, but more recent innovations include digestible insecticides that poison the fleas when they ingest the dog's blood. Alternatively, there are drops that, when placed on the back of the dog's neck, spread throughout the hair and skin to kill adult fleas.

TICKS

Though not as common as fleas, ticks are found all over the tropical and temperate world. They don't bite, like fleas; they harpoon. They dig their sharp proboscis (nose) into the dog's skin and drink the blood. Their

adult insecticides are only active for a few days.

When treating with a household spray, it is a good idea to vacuum before applying the product. This stimulates as many pupae as possible to hatch into adult fleas. The vacuum cleaner should also be treated with an insecticide to prevent the eggs and larvae that have been collected in the vacuum bag from hatching.

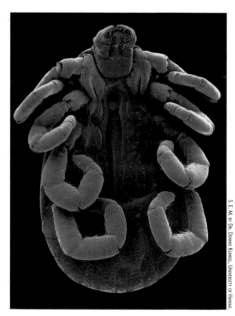

S. E. M. BY DR. DENNIS KUNKEL, UNIVERSITY OF HAWAII

only food and drink is dog's blood. Dogs can get Lyme disease, Rocky Mountain spotted fever, tick bite paralysis and many other diseases from ticks. They may live where fleas are found and they like to hide in cracks or seams in walls. They are controlled the same way fleas are controlled.

The American dog tick, *Dermacentor variabilis*, may well be the most common dog tick in many geographical areas, especially those areas where the climate is hot and humid. Most dog ticks have life expectancies of a week to six months, depending upon climatic conditions. They can neither jump nor fly, but they can crawl slowly and can range up to 16 feet to reach a sleeping or unsuspecting dog.

MITES

Just as fleas and ticks can be problematic for your dog, mites can also lead to an itchy nuisance. Microscopic in size, mites are related to ticks and generally take up permanent residence on their host animal—in this case, your dog! The term *mange* refers to any infestation caused by one of the mighty mites, of which there are six varieties that concern dog owners.

Demodex mites cause a condition known as demodicosis

DEER-TICK CROSSING

The great outdoors may be fun for your dog, but it also is an home to dangerous ticks. Deer ticks carry a bacterium known as *Borrelia burgdorferi* and are most active in the autumn and spring. When infections are caught early, penicillin and tetracycline are effective antibiotics, but if left untreated the bacteria may cause neurological, kidney and cardiac problems as well as long-term trouble with walking and painful joints.

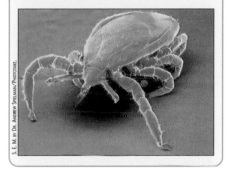

S. E. M. BY DR. ANDREW SYELLMAN/PHOTOTAKE.

PHOTO BY DR. DENNIS KUNKEL, UNIVERSITY OF HAWAII.

The head of an American dog tick, *Dermacentor variabilis*, enlarged and colorized for effect.

The mange mite, *Psoroptes bovis*, can infest cattle and other domestic animals.

PHOTO BY JAMES HAYDEN/YOAV/PHOTOTAKE

(sometimes called red mange or follicular mange), in which the mites live in the dog's hair follicles and sebaceous glands. This type of mange is commonly passed from the dam to her puppies and usually shows up on the puppies' muzzles, though demodicosis is not transferable from one normal dog to another. Most dogs recover from this type of mange without any treatment, though topical therapies are commonly prescribed by the vet.

Human lice look like dog lice; the two are closely related.

PHOTO BY DWIGHT R. KUHN.

The *Cheyletiellosis* mite is the hook-mouthed culprit associated with "walking dandruff," a condition that affects dogs as well as cats and rabbits. This mite lives on the surface of the animal's skin and is readily transferable through direct or indirect contact with an affected animal. The dandruff is present in the form of scaly skin, which may or may not be itchy. If not treated, this mange can affect a whole kennel of dogs and can be spread to humans as well.

The *Sarcoptes* mite causes intense itching on the dog in the form of a condition known as scabies or sarcoptic mange. The cycle of the *Sarcoptes* mite lasts about three weeks, and the mites live in the top layer of the dog's skin (epidermis), preferably in areas with little hair. Scabies is highly contagious and can be passed to humans. Sometimes an allergic reaction to the mite worsens the severe itching associated with sarcoptic mange.

Ear mites, *Otodectes cynotis,* lead to otodectic mange, which most commonly affects the outer ear canal of the dog, though other areas can be affected as well. Dogs with ear-mite infestation commonly scratch at their ears, causing further irritation, and shake their heads. Dark brown droppings in the outer ear confirm the diagnosis. Your vet can prescribe a treatment to flush out the ears and kill any eggs in the ears. A complete month of treatment is necessary to cure the mange.

Two other mites, less common in dogs, include *Dermanyssus gallinae* (the poultry or red mite) and *Eutrombicula alfreddugesi* (the North American mite associated with trombiculidiasis or chigger infestation). The poultry mite frequently lives on chickens, but can transfer to dogs who spend time near farm animals. Chigger infestation affects dogs in the

DO NOT MIX
Never mix parasite control products without first consulting your vet. Some products can become toxic when combined with others and can cause fatal consequences.

NOT A DROP TO DRINK
Never allow your dog to swim in polluted water or public areas where water quality can be suspect. Even perfectly clear water can harbor parasites, many of which can cause serious to fatal illnesses in canines. Areas inhabited by water-fowl and other wildlife are especially dangerous.

Central US who have exposure to woodlands. The types of mange caused by both of these mites are treatable by veterinarians.

INTERNAL PARASITES

Most animals—fishes, birds and mammals, including dogs and humans—have worms and other parasites that live inside their bodies. According to Dr. Herbert R. Axelrod, the fish pathologist, there are two kinds of parasites: dumb and smart. The smart parasites live in peaceful cooperation with their hosts (symbiosis), while the dumb parasites kill their hosts. Most worm infections are relatively easy to control. If they are not controlled, they weaken the host dog to the point that other medical problems occur, but they do not kill the host as dumb parasites would.

A brown dog tick, *Rhipicephalus sanguineus*, is an uncommon but annoying tick found on dogs.
PHOTO BY CAROLINA BIOLOGICAL SUPPLY/PHOTOTAKE.

Photo by Carolina Biological Supply/Phototake.

The roundworm *Rhabditis* can infect both dogs and humans.

ROUNDWORMS

Average-size dogs can pass 1,360,000 roundworm eggs every day. For example, if there were only 1 million dogs in the world, the world would be saturated with thousands of tons of dog feces. These feces would contain around 15,000,000,000 roundworm eggs.

Up to 31% of home yards and children's sand boxes in the US contain roundworm eggs.

Flushing dog's feces down the toilet is not a safe practice because the usual sewage treatments do not destroy roundworm eggs.

Infected puppies start shedding roundworm eggs at three weeks of age. They can be infected by their mother's milk.

The roundworm, *Ascaris lumbricoides*.

Photo by Dwight R. Kuhl.

ROUNDWORMS

The roundworms that infect dogs are known scientifically as *Toxocara canis*. They live in the dog's intestines and shed eggs continually. It has been estimated that a dog produces about 6 or more ounces of feces every day. Each ounce of feces averages hundreds of thousands of roundworm eggs. There are no known areas in which dogs roam that do not contain roundworm eggs. The greatest danger of roundworms is that they infect people, too! It is wise to have your dog tested regularly for roundworms.

In young puppies, roundworms cause bloated bellies, diarrhea, coughing and vomiting, and are transmitted from the dam (through blood or milk). Affected puppies will not appear as animated as normal puppies. The worms appear spaghetti-like, measuring as long as 6 inches. Adult dogs can acquire roundworms through coprophagia (eating contaminated feces) or by killing rodents that carry roundworms.

Roundworm infection can kill puppies and cause severe problems in adults, as the hatched larvae travel to the lungs and trachea through the bloodstream. Cleanliness is the best preventative for roundworms. Always pick up after your dog and dispose of feces in appropriate receptacles.

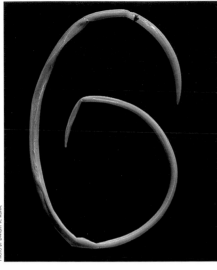

PHOTO BY DWIGHT R. KUHN.

HOOKWORMS

In the United States, dog owners have to be concerned about four different species of hookworm, the most common and most serious of which is *Ancylostoma caninum*, which prefers warm climates. The others are *Ancylostoma braziliense*, *Ancylostoma tubaeforme* and *Uncinaria stenocephala*, the latter of which is a concern to dogs living in the Northern US and Canada, as this species prefers cold climates. Hookworms are dangerous to humans as well as to dogs and cats, and can be the cause of severe anemia due to iron deficiency. The worm uses its teeth to attach itself to the dog's intestines and changes the site of its attachment about six times per day. Each time the worm repositions itself, the dog loses blood and can become anemic. *Ancylostoma caninum* is the most likely of the four species to cause anemia in the dog.

Symptoms of hookworm infection include dark stools, weight loss, general weakness, pale coloration and anemia, as well as possible skin problems. Fortunately, hookworms are easily purged from the affected dog with a number of medications that have proven effective. Discuss these with your veterinarian. Most heartworm preventatives include a hookworm insecticide as well.

Owners also must be aware that hookworms can infect humans, who can acquire the larvae through exposure to contaminated feces. Since the worms cannot complete their life cycle on a human, the worms simply infest the skin and cause irritation. This condition is known as cutaneous larva migrans syndrome. As a preventative, use disposable gloves or a "poop-scoop" to pick up your dog's droppings and prevent your dog (or neighborhood cats) from defecating in children's play areas.

The hookworm *Ancylostoma caninum*.

PHOTO BY C. JAMES WEBB/PHOTOTAKE.

The infective stage of the hookworm larva.

TAPEWORMS

Humans, rats, squirrels, foxes, coyotes, wolves and domestic dogs are all susceptible to tapeworm infection. Except in humans, tapeworms are usually not a fatal infection. Infected individuals can harbor 1000 parasitic worms.

Tapeworms, like some other types of worm, are hermaphroditic, meaning male and female in the same worm.

If dogs eat infected rats or mice, or anything else injected with tapeworm, they get the tapeworm disease. One month after attaching to a dog's intestine, the worm starts shedding eggs. These eggs are infective immediately. Infective eggs can live for a few months without a host animal.

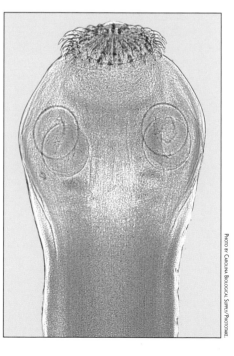

The head and rostellum (the round prominence on the scolex) of a tapeworm, which infects dogs and humans.

PHOTO BY CAROLINA BIOLOGICAL SUPPLY/PHOTOTAKE.

TAPEWORMS

There are many species of tapeworm, all of which are carried by fleas! The most common tapeworm affecting dogs is known as *Dipylidium caninum*. The dog eats the flea and starts the tapeworm cycle. Humans can also be infected with tapeworms—so don't eat fleas! Fleas are so small that your dog could pass them onto your hands, your plate or your food and thus make it possible for you to ingest a flea that is carrying tapeworm eggs.

While tapeworm infection is not life-threatening in dogs (smart parasite!), it can be the cause of a very serious liver disease for humans. About 50% of the humans infected with *Echinococcus multilocularis*, a type of tapeworm that causes alveolar hydatid, perish.

WHIPWORMS

In North America, whipworms are counted among the most common parasitic worms in dogs. The whipworm's scientific name is *Trichuris vulpis*. These worms attach themselves in the lower parts of the intestine, where they feed. Affected dogs may only experience upset tummies, colic and diarrhea. These worms, however, can live for months or years in the dog, beginning their larval stage in the small intestine, spending their adult stage in the large intestine and finally passing infective eggs through the dog's feces. The only way to detect whipworms is through a fecal examination, though this is not always foolproof. Treatment for whipworms is tricky, due to the worms' unusual life-cycle pattern, and very often dogs are reinfected due to exposure to infective eggs on the ground. The whipworm eggs can survive in the environment for as long as five years, thus cleaning up droppings in your own backyard as well as in public places is absolutely essential for sanitation purposes and the health of your dog.

THREADWORMS

Though less common than round-worms, hookworms and those listed above, threadworms concern dog owners in the Southwestern US and Gulf Coast area where the climate is hot and humid. Living in the small intestine of the dog, this worm measures a mere 2 millimeters and is round in shape. Like that of the whipworm, the threadworm's life cycle is very complex and the eggs and larvae are passed through the feces. A deadly disease in humans, Strongyloides readily infects people, and the handling of feces is the most common means of transmission. Threadworms are most often seen in young puppies; bloody diarrhea and pneumonia are symptoms. Sick puppies must be isolated and treated immediately; vets recommend a follow-up treatment one month later.

HEARTWORM PREVENTATIVES

There are many heartworm preventatives on the market, many of which are sold at your veterinarian's office. These products can be given daily or monthly, depending on the manufacturer's instructions. All of these preventatives contain chemical insecticides directed at killing heartworms, which leads to some controversy among dog owners. In effect, heartworm preventatives are necessary evils, though you should determine how necessary based on your pet's lifestyle. There is no doubt that heartworm is a dreadful disease that threatens the life of dogs. However, the likelihood of your dog's being bitten by an infected mosquito is slim in most places, and a mosquito-repellent (or an herbal remedy such as Wormwood or Black Walnut) is much safer for your dog and will not compromise his immune system (the way heartworm preventatives will). Should you decide to use the traditional preventative "medications," you can consider giving the pill every other or third month. Since the toxins in the pill will kill the heartworms at all stages of development, the pill would be effective in killing larvae, nymphs or adults and it takes four months for the larvae to reach the adult stage. Thus, there is no rationale to poisoning the dog's system on a monthly basis. Lastly, do not give the pill during the winter months since there are no mosquitoes around to pass on their infection, unless you live in a tropical environment.

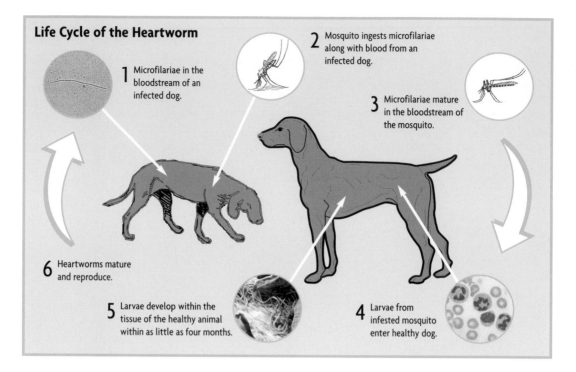

Life Cycle of the Heartworm

1 Microfilariae in the bloodstream of an infected dog.

2 Mosquito ingests microfilariae along with blood from an infected dog.

3 Microfilariae mature in the bloodstream of the mosquito.

4 Larvae from infested mosquito enter healthy dog.

5 Larvae develop within the tissue of the healthy animal within as little as four months.

6 Heartworms mature and reproduce.

HEARTWORMS

Heartworms are thin, extended worms up to 12 inches long, which live in a dog's heart and the major blood vessels surrounding it. Dogs may have up to 200 worms. Symptoms may be loss of energy, loss of appetite, coughing, the development of a pot belly and anemia.

Heartworms are transmitted by mosquitoes. The mosquito drinks the blood of an infected dog and takes in larvae with the blood. The larvae, called microfilariae, develop within the body of the mosquito and are passed on to the next dog bitten after the larvae mature. It takes two to three weeks for the larvae to develop to the infective stage within the body of the mosquito. Dogs are usually treated at about six weeks of age and maintained on a prophylactic dose given monthly.

Blood testing for heartworms is not necessarily indicative of how seriously your dog is infected. Although this is a dangerous disease, it is not easy for a dog to be infected. Discuss the various preventatives with your vet, as there are many different types now available. Together you can decide on a safe course of prevention for your dog.

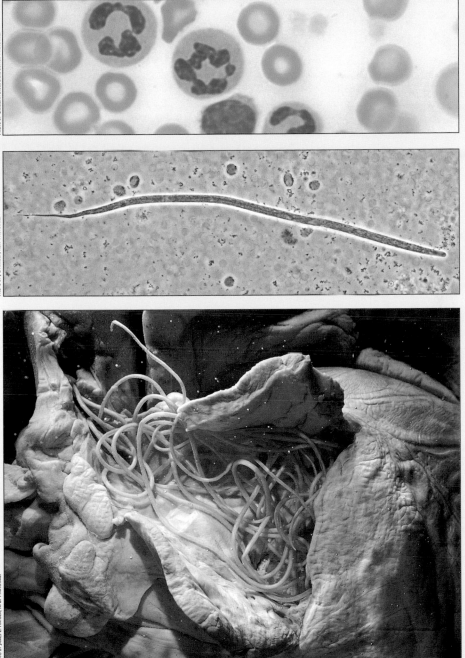

Magnified heartworm larvae, *Dirofilaria immitis.*

Photo by Carolina Biological Supply/Phototake.

Heartworm, *Dirofilaria immitis.*

Photo by J E Hayden, RBP/Phototake.

The heart of a dog infected with canine heartworm, *Dirofilaria immitis.*

Photo by James E. Hayden, RPB/Phototake.

Recognizing a Sick Dog

Unlike colicky babies and cranky children, our canine charges cannot tell us when they are feeling ill. Therefore, there are a number of signs that owners can identify to know that their dogs are not feeling well.

Take note for physical manifestations such as:

- unusual, bad odor, including bad breath
- excessive shedding
- wax in the ears, chronic ear irritation
- oily, flaky, dull haircoat
- mucus, tearing or similar discharge in the eyes
- fleas or mites
- mucus in stool, diarrhea
- sensitivity to petting or handling
- licking at paws, scratching face, etc.

Keep an eye out for behavioral changes as well including:

- lethargy, idleness
- lack of patience or general irritability
- lack of appetite
- phobias (fear of people, loud noises, etc.)
- strange behavior, suspicion, fear
- coprophagia
- more frequent barking
- whimpering, crying

Get Well Soon

You don't need a DVM to provide good TLC to your sick or recovering dog, but you do need to pay attention to some details that normally wouldn't bother him. The following tips will aid Fido's recovery and get him back on his paws again:

- Keep his space free of irritating smells, like heavy perfumes and air fresheners.
- Rest is the best medicine! Avoid harsh lighting that will prevent your dog from sleeping. Shade him from bright sunlight during the day and dim the lights in the evening.
- Keep the noise level down. Animals are more sensitive to sound when they are sick.

- Be attentive to any necessary temperature adjustments. A dog with a fever needs a cool room and cold liquids. A bitch that is whelping or recovering from surgery will be more comfortable in a warm room, consuming warm liquids and food.
- You wouldn't send a sick child back to school early, so don't rush your dog back into a full routine until he seems absolutely ready.

Disease	What is it?	What causes it?	Symptoms
Leptospirosis	Severe disease that affects the internal organs; can be spread to people.	A bacterium, which is often carried by rodents, that enters through mucous membranes and spreads quickly throughout the body.	Range from fever, vomiting and loss of appetite in less severe cases to shock, irreversible kidney damage and possibly death in most severe cases.
Rabies	Potentially deadly virus that infects warm-blooded mammals.	Bite from a carrier of the virus, mainly wild animals	1st stage: dog exhibits change in behavior, fear. 2nd stage: dog's behavior becomes more aggressive. 3rd stage: loss of coordination, trouble with bodily functions.
Parvovirus	Highly contagious virus, potentially deadly.	Ingestion of the virus, which is usually spread through the feces of infected dogs.	Most common: severe diarrhea. Also vomiting, fatigue, lack of appetite.
Kennel cough	Contagious respiratory infection.	Combination of types of bacteria and virus. Most common: *Bordetella bronchiseptica* bacteria and parainfluenza virus.	Chronic cough.
Distemper	Disease primarily affecting respiratory and nervous system.	Virus that is related to the human measles virus.	Mild symptoms such as fever, lack of appetite and mucus secretion progress to evidence of brain damage, "hard pad."
Hepatitis	Virus primarily affecting the liver.	Canine adenovirus type I (CAV-1). Enters system when dog breathes in particles.	Lesser symptoms include listlessness, diarrhea, vomiting. More severe symptoms include "blue-eye" (clumps of virus in eye).
Coronavirus	Virus resulting in digestive problems.	Virus is spread through infected dog's feces.	Stomach upset evidenced by lack of appetite, vomiting, diarrhea.

First Aid at a Glance

Burns
Place the affected area under cool water; use ice if only a small area is burnt.

Bee Stings/Insect bites
Apply ice to relieve swelling; antihistamine dosed properly.

Animal bites
Clean any bleeding area; apply pressure until bleeding subsides; go to the vet.

Spider bites
Use cold compress and a pressurized pack to inhibit venom's spreading.

Antifreeze poisoning
Immediately induce vomiting by using hydrogen peroxide.

Fish hooks
Removal best handled by vet; hook must be cut in order to remove.

Snake bites
Pack ice around bite; contact vet quickly; identify snake for proper antivenin.

Car accident
Move dog from roadway with blanket; seek veterinary aid.

Shock
Calm the dog; keep him warm; seek immediate veterinary help.

Nosebleed
Apply cold compress to the nose; apply pressure to any visible abrasion.

Bleeding
Apply pressure above the area; treat wound by applying a cotton pack.

Heat stroke
Submerge dog in cold bath; cool down with fresh air and water; go to the vet.

Frostbite/Hypothermia
Warm the dog with a warm bath, electric blankets or hot water bottles.

Abrasions
Clean the wound and wash out thoroughly with fresh water; apply antiseptic.

!! *Remember: an injured dog may attempt to bite a helping hand from fear and confusion. Always muzzle the dog before trying to offer assistance.* **!!**

Number-One Killer Disease in Dogs: CANCER

In every age there is a word associated with a disease or plague that causes humans to shudder. In the 21st century, that word is "cancer." Just as cancer is the leading cause of death in humans, it claims nearly half the lives of dogs that die from a natural disease as well as half the dogs that die over the age of ten years.

Described as a genetic disease, cancer becomes a greater risk as the dog ages. Veterinarians and dog owners have become increasingly aware of the threat of cancer to dogs. Statistics reveal that one dog in every five will develop cancer, the most common of which is skin cancer. Many cancers, including prostate, ovarian and breast cancer, can be avoided by spaying and neutering our dogs by the age of six months.

Early detection of cancer can save or extend your dog's life, so it is absolutely vital for owners to have their dogs examined by a qualified veterinarian or oncologist immediately upon detection of any abnormality. Certain dietary guidelines have also proven to reduce the onset and spread of cancer. Foods based on fish rather than beef, due to the presence of Omega-3 fatty acids, are recommended. Other amino acids such as glutamine have significant benefits for canines, particularly those breeds that show a greater susceptibility to cancer.

Cancer management and treatments promise hope for future generations of canines. Since the disease is genetic, breeders should never breed a dog whose parents, grandparents and any related siblings have developed cancer. It is difficult to know whether to exclude an otherwise healthy dog from a breeding program as the disease does not manifest itself until the dog's senior years.

RECOGNIZE CANCER WARNING SIGNS

Since early detection can possibly rescue your dog from becoming a cancer statistic, it is essential for owners to recognize the possible signs and seek the assistance of a qualified professional.

- Abnormal bumps or lumps that continue
  to grow
- Bleeding or discharge from any body cavity
- Persistent stiffness or lameness
- Recurrent sores or sores that do not heal
- Inappetence
- Breathing difficulties
- Weight loss
- Bad breath or odors
- General malaise and fatigue
- Eating and swallowing problems
- Difficulty urinating and defecating

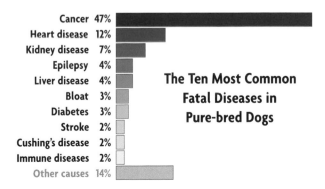

Cancer	47%
Heart disease	12%
Kidney disease	7%
Epilepsy	4%
Liver disease	4%
Bloat	3%
Diabetes	3%
Stroke	2%
Cushing's disease	2%
Immune diseases	2%
Other causes	14%

The Ten Most Common Fatal Diseases in Pure-bred Dogs

Your Senior American Pit Bull Terrier

The hardy Pit Bull usually stays active and looks fit and alert well into his senior years.

The term *old* is a qualitative term. For dogs, as well as for their masters, old is relative. Certainly we can all distinguish between a puppy Pit Bull and an adult Pit Bull—there are the obvious physical traits, such as size, appearance and facial expressions, and personality traits. Puppies and young dogs like to play with children. Children's natural exuberance is a good match for the seemingly endless energy of young dogs. They like to run, jump, chase and retrieve. When dogs grow older and cease their interaction with children, they are often thought of as being too old to keep pace with the children.

On the other hand, if a Pit Bull is only exposed to people with quieter lifestyles, his life will normally be less active and the decrease in his activity level as he ages will not be as obvious.

If people live to be 100 years old, dogs live to be 20 years old. While this might seem like a good rule of thumb, it is *very* inaccurate. When trying to compare dog years to human years, you cannot make a generalization about all dogs. You can make the generalization that 13 years is a good lifespan for an American Pit Bull Terrier. Pit Bulls generally are

GETTING OLD
The bottom line is simply that your dog is getting old when you think he is getting old because he slows down in his level of general activity, including walking, running, eating, jumping and retrieving. On the other hand, the frequency of certain activities increases, such as more sleeping, more barking and more repetition of habits like going to the door without being called when you put your coat on to leave the house.

considered physically mature within two to three years of age, or some even earlier, but can reproduce before they are fully mature. So again we will make a generalization that the first three years of a dog's life are like seven times that of comparable humans. That means a 3-year-old dog is like a 21-year-old human. However, as the different variables show, there is no hard and fast rule for comparing dog and human ages. Small breeds tend to live longer than large breeds, some breeds' adolescent periods last longer than others' and some breeds experience rapid periods of growth. The comparison is made even more difficult, for, likewise, not all humans age at the same rate...and human females usually live longer than human males.

WHAT TO LOOK FOR IN SENIORS

Most veterinarians and behaviorists use the seven-year mark as the time to consider a dog a senior. The term *senior* does not imply that the dog is geriatric and has begun to fail in mind and body. Aging is essentially a slowing process. Humans readily admit that they feel a difference in their activity level from age 20 to 30, and then from 30 to 40, etc. By treating the seven-year-old dog as a senior, owners are able to implement certain therapeutic and preventative medical strategies

with the help of their vets.

A senior-care program should include at least two veterinary visits per year and screening sessions to determine the dog's health status, as well as nutritional counseling. Veterinarians determine the senior dog's health status through a blood smear for a complete blood count, serum chemistry profile with electrolytes, urinalysis, blood pressure check, electrocardiogram, ocular tonometry (pressure on the eyeball) and dental prophylaxis.

Such an extensive program for senior dogs is well advised before owners start to see the obvious physical signs of aging, such as slower and inhibited movement, graying, increased sleep/nap periods and disinterest in play and other activity. This preventative program promises a

---

SENIOR SIGNS

An old dog starts to show one or more of the following symptoms:

- The hair on the face and paws starts to turn gray. The color breakdown usually starts around the eyes and mouth.
- Sleep patterns are deeper and longer, and the old dog is harder to awaken.
- Food intake diminishes.
- Responses to calls, whistles and other signals are ignored more and more.
- Eye contact does not evoke tail wagging (assuming it once did).

longer, healthier life for the aging dog. Among the physical problems common in aging dogs are the loss of sight and hearing, arthritis, kidney and liver failure, diabetes mellitus, heart disease and Cushing's disease (a hormonal disease).

In addition to the physical manifestations discussed, there are some behavioral changes and problems related to aging dogs. Dogs suffering from hearing or vision loss, dental discomfort or arthritis can become aggressive. Likewise, the near-deaf and/or blind dog may be startled more easily and react in an unexpectedly aggressive manner. Seniors suffering from senility can become more impatient and irritable. Housesoiling accidents are associated with loss of mobility, kidney problems and loss of sphincter control as well as plaque accumulation, physiological brain changes and reactions to medications. Older dogs, just like young puppies, can suffer from separation anxiety, which can lead to excessive barking, whining, housesoiling and destructive behavior. Seniors may become fearful of everyday sounds, such as vacuum cleaners, heaters, thunder and passing traffic. Some dogs have difficulty sleeping, due to discomfort, the need for frequent outside visits and the like.

Owners should avoid spoiling the older dog with too many fatty

---

NOTICING THE SYMPTOMS
The symptoms listed below are symptoms that gradually appear and become more noticeable. They are not life-threatening; however, the symptoms below are to be taken very seriously and warrant a discussion with your veterinarian:
- Your dog drinks more water and urinates more frequently. Wetting and bowel accidents take place indoors without warning.
- Vomiting becomes more and more frequent.
- Your dog cries and whimpers when he moves, and he stops running completely.
- Convulsions start or become more serious and frequent. The usual convulsion (spasm) is when the dog stiffens and starts to tremble, being unable or unwilling to move. The seizure usually lasts for 5 to 30 minutes.

---

treats. Obesity is a common problem in older dogs and subtracts years from their lives. Keep the senior dog as trim as possible, since excessive weight puts additional stress on the body's vital organs. Some breeders recommend supplementing the diet with foods high in fiber and lower in calories. Adding fresh vegetables and marrow broth to the senior's diet makes a tasty, low-calorie, low-fat supplement. Vets also offer specialty diets for senior dogs that are worth exploring.

TALK IT OUT
The more openly your family discusses the whole stressful occurrence of the aging and eventual loss of a beloved pet, the easier it will be for you when the time comes.

Your dog, as he nears his twilight years, needs your patience and good care more than ever. Never punish an older dog for an accident or abnormal behavior. For all the years of love, protection and companionship that your dog has provided, he deserves special attention and courtesies. The older dog may need to relieve himself at 3 a.m. because he can no longer hold it for eight hours. Older dogs may not be able to remain crated for more than two or three hours. It may be time to give up a sofa or chair to your old friend. Although he may not seem as enthusiastic about your attention and petting, he does appreciate the considerations you offer as he gets older.

Your Pit Bull does not understand why his world is slowing down. Owners must make their dogs' transition into their golden years as pleasant and rewarding as possible.

WHAT TO DO WHEN THE TIME COMES
You are never fully prepared to make a rational decision about putting your dog to sleep. It is very obvious that you love your Pit Bull or you would not be reading this book. Putting a beloved dog to sleep is extremely difficult. It is a decision that must be made with your veterinarian. You are usually forced to make the decision when your dog experiences one or more life-threatening

There are pet cemeteries that cater to dog owners who want to memorialize their beloved pets.

symptoms that have become serious enough for you to seek veterinary assistance.

If the prognosis of the malady indicates that the end is near and that your beloved pet will only continue to suffer and experience no enjoyment for the balance of his life, then euthanasia is the right choice.

WHAT IS EUTHANASIA?

Euthanasia derives from the Greek, meaning *good death. In* other words, it means the planned, painless killing of a dog suffering from a painful, incurable condition, or who is so aged that he cannot walk, see, eat or control his excretory functions. Euthanasia is usually accomplished by injection with an overdose of anesthesia or a barbiturate. Aside from the prick of the needle, the experience is usually painless.

Burial in a pet cemetery or a marker in your yard are options for memorializing a pet dog.

COCO CREME
1973 — 1989
SLOOPY
1965 — 1973

MAKING THE DECISION

The decision to euthanize your dog is never easy. The days during which the dog becomes ill and the end occurs can be unusually stressful for you. If this is your first experience with the death of a loved one, you may need the comfort dictated by your religious beliefs. If you are the head of the family and have children, you should involve them in the decision of putting your Pit Bull to sleep. Usually your dog can be maintained on drugs for a few days in order to give you ample time to make a decision. During this time, talking with members of your family or with people who have lived through the same experience can ease the burden of your inevitable decision.

THE FINAL RESTING PLACE

Dogs can have some of the same privileges as humans. The remains of your beloved dog can be buried in a pet cemetery, which is generally expensive. Alternatively, your dog can be cremated individually and the ashes returned to you. A less expensive option is mass cremation, although, of course, the ashes cannot then be returned. Vets can usually help you locate a nearby pet cemetery or arrange the cremation on your behalf. The cost of these options should always be discussed frankly and openly with your veterinarian.

CDS: COGNITIVE DYSFUNCTION SYNDROME
"OLD-DOG SYNDROME"

There are many ways to evaluate old-dog syndrome. Vets have defined CDS (cognitive dysfunction syndrome) as the gradual deterioration of cognitive abilities. These are indicated by changes in the dog's behavior. When a dog changes his routine response, and maladies have been eliminated as the cause of these behavioral changes, then CDS is the usual diagnosis.

More than half of the dogs over eight years old suffer from some form of CDS. The older the dog, the more chance he has of suffering from CDS. In humans, doctors often dismiss the CDS behavioral changes as part of "winding down."

There are four major signs of CDS: frequent potty accidents inside the home, sleeping much more or much less than normal, acting confused and failing to respond to social stimuli.

SYMPTOMS OF CDS

FREQUENT POTTY ACCIDENTS
- *Urinates in the house.*
- *Defecates in the house.*
- *Doesn't signal that he wants to go out.*

SLEEP PATTERNS
- *Moves much more slowly.*
- *Sleeps more than normal during the day.*
- *Sleeps less during the night.*

CONFUSION
- *Goes outside and just stands there.*
- *Appears confused with a faraway look in his eyes.*
- *Hides more often.*
- *Doesn't recognize friends.*
- *Doesn't come when called.*
- *Walks around listlessly and without a destination.*

FAILURE TO RESPOND TO SOCIAL STIMULI
- *Comes to people less frequently, whether called or not.*
- *Doesn't tolerate petting for more than a short time.*
- *Doesn't come to the door when you return home.*

It's amazing what your agile Pit Bull will do for a snack.

Behavior of Your American Pit Bull Terrier

As a Pit Bull owner, you have selected your dog so that you and your loved ones can have a companion, a protector, a friend and a four-legged family member. You invest time, money and effort to care for and train the family's new charge. Of course, this chosen canine behaves perfectly! Well, perfectly like a *dog*.

THINK LIKE A DOG

Dogs do not think like humans, nor do humans think like dogs, though we try. Unfortunately, a dog is incapable of figuring out how humans think, so the responsibility falls on the owner to try to adopt a viable canine mindset. Dogs cannot rationalize and exist in the present moment. Many a dog owner makes the mistake in training of thinking that he can reprimand his dog for something the dog did a while ago. Basically, you cannot even reprimand a dog for something he did 20 seconds ago! Either catch him in the act or

Pit Bull Terriers are intelligent animals and they can readily learn and understand commands. After all, they were bred for their ability to follow instruction from their masters.

forget it! It is a waste of your and your dog's time—in his mind, you are reprimanding him for whatever he is doing at that moment.

The following behavioral problems represent some which owners most commonly encounter. Every dog is unique and every situation is unique. No author could purport for you to solve your Pit Bull's problem simply by reading a chapter in a breed book. Here we outline some basic "dogspeak" so that owners' chances of solving behavioral problems are increased. Discuss bad habits with your vet and he can recommend a behavioral

DOGGIE DEMOCRACY
Your dog inherited the pack-leader mentality. He only knows about pecking order. He instinctively wants to be "top dog," but you have to convince him that you are boss. There is no such thing as living in a democracy with your dog. You are the one who makes the rules.

specialist to consult in appropriate cases. Since behavioral abnormalities are the leading reason for owners' abandoning their pets, we hope that you will make a valiant effort to solve your Pit

A dog of any breeds can show possessive tendencies toward his toys. It's not advised to try to take a toy away from a dog.

Body language is a sure sign of what a dog is thinking. This pup's pose means he's ready to play.

Bull's problem. Patience and understanding are virtues that must dwell in every pet-loving household.

AGGRESSION

Aggression can be a very big problem in dogs. Aggression, when not controlled, becomes dangerous. An aggressive dog, no matter the size, may lunge at, bite or even attack a person or another dog. Aggressive behavior is not to be tolerated. It is more than just inappropriate behavior; it is not safe, especially with a powerful breed such as the Pit Bull. It is painful for a family to watch their dog become unpredictable in his

DEALING WITH AGGRESSION

The American Pit Bull Terrier has been the target of much breed-specific legislation, but steps are being taken to document incidences of canine aggression more clearly so that entire breeds are not punished unfairly. An outwardly aggressive Pit Bull is the result of irresponsible ownership, yet it is the breed that suffers due to the negative publicity one incident can generate. Dog aggression, regardless of the breed, is a growing problem that must be addressed. The current focus is on enacting laws that put the responsibility on dog owners to train and keep their dogs under control.

behavior to the point where they are afraid of the dog. And while not all aggressive behavior is dangerous, it can be frightening: growling, baring teeth, etc. It is important to get to the root of the problem to ascertain why the dog is acting in this manner. Aggression is a display of dominance, and the dog should not have the dominant role in his pack, which is, in this case, your family.

It is important not to challenge an aggressive dog as this could provoke an attack. Observe your Pit Bull's body language. Does he make direct eye contact and stare? Does he try to make himself as large as possible: ears pricked, chest out, tail erect? Height and size signify authority in a dog pack—being taller or "above" another dog literally means that he

> **PROFESSIONAL TRAINING**
> If your dog barks menacingly or growls at strangers, or if he growls at anyone who comes near while he is eating, playing with a toy or taking a rest in his favorite spot, he needs proper professional training because sooner or later this behavior can result in someone's being bitten.

is "above" in the social status. These body signals tell you that your Pit Bull thinks he is in charge, a problem that needs to be dealt with. An aggressive dog is unpredictable in that you never know when he is going to strike and what he is going to do. You cannot understand why a dog that is playful and loving one minute is growling and snapping the next.

When dogs meet, their sniffing each other is a natural way of getting to know each other.

The dominant dog is the one that gets the bone!

Fear is a common cause of aggression in dogs. If you can isolate what brings out the fear reaction, you can help the dog get over it. Supervise your Pit Bull's interactions with people and other dogs, and praise the dog when it goes well. If he starts to act aggressively in a situation, correct him and remove him from the situation. Do not let people approach the dog and start petting him without your express permission. That way, you can have the dog sit to accept petting, and praise him when he behaves properly. You are focusing on praise and on modifying his behavior by rewarding him when he acts appropriately. By being gentle and by supervising his interactions, you are showing him that there is no need to be afraid or defensive.

The best solution is to consult a behavioral specialist, one who has experience with the Pit Bull if possible. Together, perhaps you can pinpoint the cause of your dog's aggression and do something about it. An aggressive dog cannot be trusted, and a dog that cannot be trusted is not safe to have as a family pet. If the pet Pit Bull becomes untrustworthy, he

Show your dog who is boss! Training your Pit Bull to wait for his food shows him that you are in control, not him.

FEAR IN A GROWN DOG

Fear in a grown dog is often the result of improper or incomplete socialization as a pup, or it can be the result of a traumatic experience he suffered when young. Keep in mind that the term "traumatic" is relative—something that you would not think twice about can leave a lasting negative impression on a puppy. If the dog experiences a similar experience later in life, he may try to fight back to protect himself. Again, this behavior is very unpredictable, especially if you do not know what is triggering his fear.

cannot be kept in the home with the family. The family must get rid of the dog. In the *very* worst case, the dog must be euthanized.

AGGRESSION TOWARD OTHER DOGS

A Pit Bull's aggressive behavior toward another dog stems from the breed's fighting-dog ancestry as well as from not enough exposure to other dogs at an early age. If other dogs make your Pit Bull nervous and agitated, he will lash out as a protective mechanism. A dog who has not received sufficient exposure to other canines tends to believe that he is the only dog on the planet. The animal becomes so dominant that he does not even show signs that he is fearful or threatened. Without growling or any other physical signal as a warning, he will lunge at and bite the other dog.

A way to correct this is to let your Pit Bull approach another dog when walking on leash. Watch very closely and at the very first sign of aggression, correct your Pit Bull and pull him away. Scold him for any sign of discomfort, and then praise him when he ignores or tolerates the other dog. Keep this up until either he stops the aggressive behavior, learns to ignore the other dog or even accepts other dogs. Praise him lavishly for his correct behavior.

DOMINANT AGGRESSION

A social hierarchy is firmly established in a wild dog pack. The dog wants to dominate those under him and please those above him. Dogs know that there must be a leader. If you are not the obvious choice for emperor, the dog will assume the throne! These conflicting innate desires are what a dog owner is up against when he sets about training a dog. In training a dog to obey commands, the owner is

A dog's rolling on his back and exposing his belly is a submissive posture.

The Pit Bull is not the best choice for a multiple-dog household, especially for first-time owners, but many breed fanciers keep more than one Pit Bull successfully.

reinforcing that he is the top dog in the "pack" and that the dog should, and should want to, serve his superior. Thus, the owner is suppressing the dog's urge to dominate by modifying his behavior and making him obedient.

An important part of training is taking every opportunity to reinforce that you are the leader. The simple action of making your Pit Bull sit to wait for his food instead of allowing him to run up to get it when he wants it says that you control when he eats; he is dependent on you for food. Although it may be difficult, do not give in to your dog's wishes every time he whines at you or looks at you with pleading eyes. It is a constant effort to show the dog that his place in

the pack is at the bottom. This is not meant to sound cruel or inhumane. You love your Pit Bull and you should treat him with care and affection. You (hopefully) did

MOMMY DEAREST

If you have decided to breed your bitch, or are already getting close to the birthing day, be aware that maternal aggression toward pups is a normal activity and should not cause panic. Biting or snapping at pups is disciplinary. It is a way for a mother to teach her pups the limits of bad behavior as well as the best ways for them to survive as canines. Cannibalism, while far more aggressive, is normal behavior for a bitch when a pup is stillborn or dies shortly after birth, or even sometimes if she is not allowed to bond with her pups.

not get a dog just so you could control another creature. Dog training is not about being cruel or feeling important, it is about molding the dog's behavior into what is acceptable and teaching him to live by your rules. In theory, it is quite simple: catch him in appropriate behavior and reward him for it. Add a dog into the equation and it becomes a bit more trying, but as a rule of thumb, positive reinforcement is what works best.

With a dominant dog, punishment and negative reinforcement can have the opposite effect of what you are after. It can make a dog fearful and/or act out aggressively if he feels he is being challenged. Remember, a dominant dog perceives himself at the top of the social heap and will fight to defend his perceived status. The best way to prevent that is to never give him reason to think that he is in control in the first place.

If you are having trouble training your Pit Bull and it seems as if he is constantly challenging your authority, seek the help of an obedience trainer or behavioral specialist. A professional will work with both you and your dog to teach you effective techniques to use at home. Beware of trainers who rely on excessively harsh methods; scolding is necessary now and then, but the focus in your training should *always* be on positive reinforcement.

SEXUAL BEHAVIOR

Dogs exhibit certain sexual behaviors that may have influenced your choice of male or female when you first purchased your Pit Bull. Spaying/neutering will eliminate most of these behaviors, but if you are purchasing a dog that you wish to show or breed, you should be aware of what you will have to deal with throughout the dog's life.

Female dogs usually have two estruses per year, each season lasting about three weeks. These

---

THE MIGHTY MALE

Males, whether castrated or not, will mount almost anything: a pillow, your leg or, much to your dismay, even your neighbor's leg. As with other types of inappropriate behavior, the dog must be corrected while in the act, which for once is not difficult. Often he will not let go! While a puppy is experimenting with his very first urges, his owners feel he needs to "sow his oats" and allow the pup to mount. As the pup grows into a full-size dog, with full-size urges, it becomes a nuisance and an embarrassment. Males always appear as if they are trying to "save the race," more determined and stronger than imaginable. While neutering the dog at an appropriate age will limit the dog's desire, it usually does not remove it entirely.

A Pit Bull's natural tendency is to show aggression toward other dogs. Always keep your Pit Bull on a strong leash whenever you are in a public place.

NO KISSES
We all love our dogs and our dogs love us. They show their love and affection by licking us. This is not a very sanitary practice, as dogs lick and sniff in some unsavory places. Kissing your dog on the mouth is strictly forbidden, as parasites can be transmitted in this manner.

heat cycle, it is not uncommon for her to experience a false pregnancy, in which her mammary glands swell and she exhibits maternal tendencies toward toys or other objects.

Owners must also recognize that mounting, a rather common behavior, is not merely a sexual expression but also one of dominance seen in males and females alike. Be consistent and persistent and you will find that you can "move mounters."

CHEWING
The national canine pastime is chewing! Every dog loves to sink his "canines" into a tasty bone. If a bone's not available, he'll sink his teeth into whatever he can. Dogs need to chew, to massage their gums, to make their new teeth feel better and to exercise their jaws. This is a natural behavior deeply imbedded in all things canine. Our role as owners is not to stop chewing, but to redirect it to positive, chew-worthy objects. Be an informed owner and purchase proper chew toys for your Pit Bull, like strong nylon bones made for large dogs. Be sure that the devices are safe and durable, since your dog's safety is at risk.

Again, the owner is responsible for ensuring a dog-proof environment. The best answer is prevention: that is, put your

are the only times in which a female dog will mate, and she usually will not allow this until the second week of the cycle. If a bitch is not bred during the

NO JUMPING

Stop a dog from jumping up before he jumps. If he is getting ready to jump onto you, simply walk away. If he jumps up on you before you can turn away, lift your knee so that it bumps him in the chest. Do not be forceful. Your dog soon will realize that jumping up is not a productive way of getting attention.

shoes, handbags and other tasty objects in their proper places (out of the reach of the growing canine mouth). Direct puppies to their toys whenever you see them tasting the furniture legs or your pant leg. Make a loud noise to attract the pup's attention and immediately escort him to his chew toy and engage him with the toy for at least four minutes, praising and encouraging him all the while.

Some trainers recommend deterrents, such as hot pepper or another bitter spice or a product designed for this purpose, to discourage the dog from chewing on unwanted objects. This is sometimes reliable, though not as often as the manufacturers of such products claim. Test out the product with your own dog before investing in a case of it.

JUMPING UP

Jumping up is a dog's friendly way of saying hello! Some dog

owners do not mind when their dog jumps up, which is fine for them. The problem arises when guests come to the house and the dog greets them in the same manner—whether they like it or not! However friendly the greeting may be, chances are your visitors will not appreciate nearly being knocked over by an overly enthusiastic Pit Bull. The dog will not be able to distinguish upon whom he can jump and whom he cannot. Therefore, it is probably best to discourage this behavior entirely.

Pick a command such as "Off" (avoid using "Down" since you will use that for the dog to lie down) and tell him "Off" when he jumps up. Place him on the ground on all fours and have him sit, praising him the whole

Dogs need to chew. Be sure they have something safe to chew on—something they find in the yard may not be good for them.

time. Always lavish him with praise and petting when he is in the sit position. That way you are still giving him a warm affectionate greeting, because you are as pleased to see him as he is to see you!

SMILE!

Dogs and humans may be the only creatures that smile. A dog will imitate the smile on his owner's face when he greets a friend. The dog only smiles at his human friends; he never smiles at another dog or cat. Usually, a dog rolls up his lips and shows his teeth in a clenched mouth while rolling over onto his back, begging for a soft scratch.

DIGGING

Digging, which is seen as a destructive behavior to humans, is actually quite a natural behavior in dogs. Digging is most closely associated with the "earth dogs" (also known as terriers), though any dog's desire to dig can be irrepressible and most frustrating to his owners. When digging occurs in your yard, it is actually a normal behavior redirected into something the dog can do in his everyday life. For example, in the wild a dog would be actively seeking food, making his own shelter, etc. He would be using his paws in a purposeful manner; he would be using them for his survival. Since you provide him with food and shelter, he has no need to use his paws for these purposes, and so the energy that he would be using manifests itself in the form of little holes all over your yard and flower beds.

Perhaps your dog is digging as a reaction to boredom—it is somewhat similar to someone eating a whole bag of chips in front of the TV—because they are there and there is not anything better to do! Basically, the answer is to provide the dog with adequate play and exercise so that his mind and paws are occupied, and so that he feels as if he is doing something useful.

Of course, digging is easiest to control if it is stopped as soon as possible, but it is often hard to

Jumping up is usually just a dog's way of saying a friendly hello.

catch a dog in the act, especially if he is alone in the yard during the day. If your dog is a compulsive digger and is not easily distracted by other activities, you can designate an area on your property where it is okay for him to dig. If you catch him digging in an off-limits area of the yard, immediately bring him to the approved area and praise him for digging there. Keep a close eye on him so that you can catch him; that is the only way he is going to

SOUND BITES

When a dog bites, there should be a good reason for his doing so. Many dogs are trained to protect a person, an area or an object. When that person, area or object is violated, the dog will attack. A dog attacks with his mouth. He has no other means of attack.

Fighting dogs (and there are many breeds other than the Pit Bull that fight) are taught to fight, but they also have a natural instinct to fight. This instinct is normally reserved for other dogs, though unfortunate accidents can occur; due to irresponsible owners and the failure to train their dogs properly.

If a dog is a biter for seemingly no reason, if he bites the hand that feeds him or if he snaps at members of your family, see your veterinarian or behaviorist immediately to learn how to modify the dog's behavior.

understand what is permitted and what is not. If you bring him to a hole he dug an hour ago and tell him "No," he will understand that you are not fond of holes, dirt or flowers. If you catch him while he is stifle-deep in your tulips, that is when he will get your message.

BARKING

Dogs cannot talk—oh, what they would say if they could! Instead, barking is a dog's way of "talking." It can be somewhat frustrating because it is not always easy to tell what a dog means by his bark—is he excited, happy, frightened, angry? Whatever it is that the dog is trying to say, he should not be punished for barking. It is only when the barking becomes excessive, and when the excessive barking becomes a bad habit, that the behavior needs to be modified.

If an intruder came into your home in the middle of the night and your Pit Bull barked a warning, wouldn't you be pleased? You would probably deem your dog a hero, a wonderful guardian and protector of the home. On the other hand, if a friend drops by unexpectedly and rings the doorbell and is greeted with a sudden sharp bark, you would probably be annoyed at the dog. But isn't it just the same behavior? The dog does not know any better...unless he sees who is at the door and it

Pit Bulls are alert and observant dogs. Being protective of home and family, they will use their barks to ward off possible intruders.

is someone he is familiar with, he will bark as a means of vocalizing that his (and your) territory is being threatened. While your friend is not posing a threat, it is all the same to the dog. Barking is his means of letting you know that there is an intrusion, whether friend or foe, on your property. This type of barking is instinctive and should not be discouraged.

Excessive habitual barking, however, is a problem that should be corrected early on. As your Pit Bull grows up, you will be able to tell when his barking is purposeful and when it is for no reason. You will become able to distinguish your dog's different barks and with what they are associated. For example, the bark when someone comes to the door will be different from the bark when he is excited to see you. It is similar to a person's tone of voice, except that the dog has to rely totally on tone of voice because he does not have the benefit of

IT'S PLAY TIME
Physical games like tug-of-war, wrestling, jumping and teasing should not be encouraged. Inciting a dog's crazy behavior tends to confuse him. The owner has to be able to control his dog at all times. Even in play, your dog has to know that you are the leader.

using words. An incessant barker will be evident at an early age.

There are some things that encourage a dog to bark. For example, if your dog barks non-stop for a few minutes and you give him a treat to quiet him, he believes that you are rewarding him for barking. He will associate barking with getting a treat, and will keep doing it until he is rewarded. On the other hand, if you give him a "Quiet" command and reward him *after* he has stopped barking, he will understand that being quiet is what you want him to do.

FOOD STEALING

Is your dog devising ways of stealing food from your counter tops? If so, you must answer the following questions: Is your Pit Bull hungry, or is he "constantly famished" like every other chow hound? Why is there food on the counter top? Face it, some dogs are more food-motivated than others; some dogs are totally obsessed by a slab of brisket and can only think of their next meal. Food stealing is terrific fun and always yields a great reward— FOOD, glorious food.

The owner's goal, therefore, is to make the "reward" less reward-ing, even startling! Plant a shaker can (an empty soda can with coins inside) on the counter so that it catches your pooch offguard. There are other devices

---

> **DISCOURAGE DOMINANCE**
>
> Never allow your puppy to growl at you or bare his tiny teeth. Such behav-ior is dominant and aggressive. If not corrected, the dog will repeat the behavior, which will become more threatening as he grows larger and will eventually lead to biting.

---

available that will surprise the dog when he is looking for a mid-afternoon snack. Such remote-control devices, though not the first choice of some trainers, allow the correction to come from the object instead of the owner. These devices are also useful to keep the snacking hound from napping on furniture that is forbidden.

BEGGING

Just like food stealing, begging is a favorite pastime of hungry puppies, with that same reward— *food*! Dogs quickly learn that their owners keep the "good food" for themselves, and that we humans do not dine on kibble alone. Begging is a conditioned response related to a specific stimulus, time and place. The sounds of the kitchen, cans and bottles opening, crinkling bags, the smell of food in preparation, etc., will excite the chow hound and soon the paws are in the air!

Here is the solution to stop-ping this behavior: Never give in to a beggar! You are rewarding the dog for sitting pretty, jumping up, whining and rubbing his nose into you by giving him that glorious reward—food.

By ignoring the dog, you will (eventually) force the behavior into extinction. Note that the behavior likely gets worse before it disappears, so be sure there are not any "softies" in the family who will give in to little "Oliver" every time he whimpers, "More, please."

SEPARATION ANXIETY
Your Pit Bull may howl, whine or otherwise vocalize his displeasure at your leaving the house and his being left alone. This is a normal case of separation anxiety, but there are things that can be done to eliminate this problem. Your dog needs to learn that he will be fine on his own for a while and that he will not wither away if he is not attended to every minute of the day. In fact, constant attention can lead to separation anxiety in the first place. If you are endlessly coddling and cooing over your dog, he will come to expect this from you all of the time and it will be more traumatic for him when you are not there. Obviously, you enjoy spending time with your dog, and he thrives on your love and attention. However, it should not become a dependent relationship in which he is heartbroken without you.

One thing you can do to minimize separation anxiety is to make your entrances and exits as low-key as possible. Do not give your dog a long drawn-out goodbye, and do not lavish him with hugs and kisses when you return. This is giving in to the attention

"LONELY WOLF"
The number of dogs that suffer from separation anxiety is on the rise as more and more pet owners find themselves at work all day. New attention is being paid to this problem, which is especially hard to diagnose since it is only evident when the dog is alone. Research is currently being done to help educate dog owners about separation anxiety and how they can help minimize this problem in their dogs

SET AN EXAMPLE
Never scream, shout, jump or run about if you want your dog to stay calm. You set the example for your dog's behavior in most circumstances. Learn from your dog's reaction to your behavior and act accordingly.

that he craves, and it will only make him miss it more when you are away. Another thing you can try is to give your dog a treat when you leave; this will not only keep him occupied and keep his mind off the fact that you just left, but it will also help him associate your leaving with a pleasant experience.

You may have to accustom your dog to being left alone in intervals, much like when you introduced your pup to his crate. Of course, when your dog starts whimpering as you approach the door, your first instinct will be to run to him and comfort him, but

do not do it! Eventually he will adjust and be just fine if you take it in small steps. His anxiety stems from being placed in an unfamiliar situation; by familiarizing him with being alone, he will learn that he is okay. That is not to say that you should purposely leave your dog home alone, but the dog needs to know that, while he can depend on you for his care, you do not have to be by his side 24 hours a day.

When the dog is alone in the house, he should be confined to his crate or a designated dog-proof area of the house. This should be the area in which he sleeps, so he should already feel comfortable there, which should make him feel more at ease when he is alone. This is just one of the many examples in which a crate is an invaluable tool for you and your dog, and another reinforcement of why your dog should view his crate as a "happy" place, a place of his own.

COPROPHAGIA
Feces eating is, to humans, one of the most disgusting behaviors that a dog could engage in, yet to the dog it is perfectly normal. It is hard for us to understand why a dog would want to eat its own feces; he could be seeking certain nutrients that are missing from his diet, he could be just plain hungry, or he could be attracted by the pleasing (to a

dog) scent. While coprophagia most often refers to the dog's eating his own feces, a dog may likely eat that of another animal as well if he comes across it. Dogs often find the stool of cats and horses more palatable than that of other dogs.

Vets have found that diets with a low digestibility, containing relatively low levels of fiber and high levels of starch, increase coprophagia. Therefore, high-fiber diets may decrease the likelihood of dogs' eating feces. Both the consistency of the stool (how firm it feels in the dog's mouth) and the presence of undigested nutrients increase the likelihood. Once the dog develops diarrhea from feces eating, he will likely quit this distasteful habit, since dogs tend to prefer eating harder feces.

To discourage this behavior, first make sure that the food you are feeding your dog is nutritionally complete and that he is getting enough food. If changes in his diet do not seem to work, and no medical cause can be found, you will have to modify the behavior through environmental control before it becomes a habit. There are some tricks you can try, such as adding an unpleasant-tasting substance to the feces to make them unpalatable or adding something to the dog's food that will make it unpleasant-tasting after it passes

Never fail to clean up your dog's droppings, even if they occur in your own yard. Your pet shop has accessories to assist you in this necessary task.

through the dog. The best way to prevent your dog from eating his stool is to make it unavailable—clean up after he eliminates and remove any stool from the garden. If it is not there, he cannot eat it.

Never reprimand the dog for stool eating, as this rarely impresses the dog. Vets recommend distracting the dog while he is in the act of stool eating. Another option is to muzzle the dog when he is in the yard to relieve himself; this usually is effective within 30 to 60 days. Coprophagia most frequently is seen in pups 6 to 12 months of age and usually disappears around the dog's first birthday.

INDEX

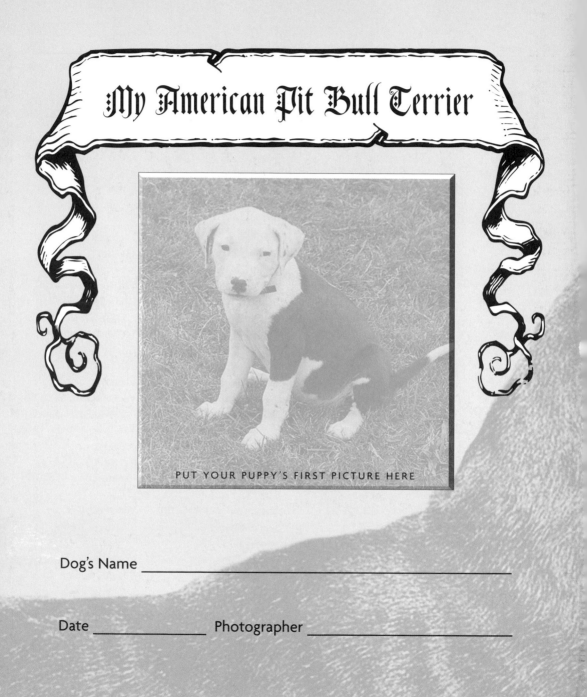

My American Pit Bull Terrier

PUT YOUR PUPPY'S FIRST PICTURE HERE

Dog's Name _____

Date _____ Photographer _____